AN ILLUSTRATED HISTORY OF THE
LATER CRUSADES

THE CRUSADES OF 1200–1588 IN PALESTINE, SPAIN, ITALY AND NORTHERN
EUROPE, FROM THE SACK OF CONSTANTINOPLE TO THE CRUSADES AGAINST
THE HUSSITES, DEPICTED IN 150 FINE ART IMAGES

CHARLES PHILLIPS

southwater

This edition is published by Southwater, an imprint of Anness Publishing Ltd, Blaby Road, Wigston, Leicestershire LE18 4SE

info@anness.com

www.southwaterbooks.com;
www.annesspublishing.com

Anness Publishing has a picture agency outlet for images for publishing, promotions or advertising. For more information, please visit www.practicalpictures.com

Publisher: Joanna Lorenz
Editorial Director: Helen Sudell
Executive Editor: Joanne Rippin
Designer: Nigel Partridge
Jacket Design: Adelle Morris
Production Controller: Bessie Bai

ETHICAL TRADING POLICY
At Anness Publishing we believe that business should be conducted in an ethical and ecologically sustainable way, with respect for the environment and a proper regard to the replacement of the natural resources we employ.
As a publisher, we use a lot of wood pulp in high-quality paper for printing, and that wood commonly comes from spruce trees. We are therefore currently growing more than 750,000 trees in three Scottish forest plantations: Berrymoss (130 hectares/320 acres), West Touxhill (125 hectares/ 305 acres) and Deveron Forest (75 hectares/185 acres). The forests we manage contain more than 3.5 times the number of trees employed each year in making paper for the books we manufacture.
Because of this ongoing ecological investment programme, you, as our customer, can have the pleasure and reassurance of knowing that a tree is being cultivated on your behalf to naturally replace the materials

used to make the book you are holding. Our forestry programme is run in accordance with the UK Woodland Assurance Scheme (UKWAS) and will be certified by the internationally recognized Forest Stewardship Council (FSC). The FSC is a non-government organization dedicated to promoting responsible management of the world's forests. Certification ensures forests are managed in an environmentally sustainable and socially responsible way. For further information about this scheme, go to www.annesspublishing.com/trees

A CIP catalogue record for this book is available from the British Library.

Previously published as part of a larger volume, *Crusades and the Crusader Knights*

PICTURE ACKNOWLEDGEMENTS
ART ARCHIVE, pp6, 8t, 10, 11, 12, 13t, 14t & b, 15, 16t, 17b, 19b, 19t & b, 20t, 22, 23t, 27tl, 28tl, 28t, 29t, 30t, 32t, 34b, 35, 36t, 36b, 37t & b, 39b, 40t & b, 41b, 42b, 43, 44, 46t, 48b, 50, 51, 52b, 53tl & tr, 55t, 56, 57b, 58bl, 58t & br, 59b, & t, 60b, 61b, 62bl, & t, 64bl, 62t & b, 64t, 65t, 68b, 69t & b, 70t & b, 71b & t, 72bl & t, 73t & b, 75, 76t & b, 77b, 78b, 79t & b, 80b & t, 81t & b, 82t & b, 83, 85t, 88b, 90b & t, 91, 92t, 94b,

BRIDGEMAN ART LIBRARY: pp1, 2t & br, 4, 6, 8t, 10, 11, 12, 13t, 14t & b, 15, 16t, 17b, 19b & t, 20t, 22, 23t, 27tl, 28tl & t, 29t, 30t, 32t, 34b, 35, 36t & b, 37t & b, 39b, 40t & b, 41b, 42b, 43, 44, 46t, 48b, 50, 51, 52b, 53tl & tr, 55t, 56, 57b, 58bl, 58t, 58br, 59b, 59t, 60b, 61b, 62bl & t, 64bl, t & b, 65t, 68b, 69t & b, 70t & b, 71b & t, 72bl & t, 73t & b, 75, 76t & b, 77b, 78b, 79t & b, 80b & t, 81t & b, 82t & b, 83, 85t, 88b, 90b & t, 91, 92t, 94b.
AKG 1t, 4t, 6, 16b, 17t, 18t, 21b, 24, 28b, 29b, 31b, 33, 34t, 39t, 42t, 45, 47t, 47r, 55bl & br, 62br, 65bl, 66b & t, 67tl & b, 87t & b, 89lb.
ANCIENT ART AND ARCHITECTURE: 9b, 31b, 65br.

ISTOCK: pp32b, 63tl, 85b.

CONTENTS

INTRODUCTION

In November 1199, at a splendid chivalric tournament at Ecry-sur-Aisne, France, Count Theobald of Champagne and Count Louis of Blois committed themselves to fight a crusade aimed at liberating the Muslim-controlled city of Jerusalem. Pope Innocent III had called the crusade in August 1198, and Counts Theobald and Louis were responding to a stirring sermon by the French priest Fulk of Neuilly, appointed by the pope to preach the crusade.

This was the fourth in a series of wars beginning in 1095, fought in the name of Christ against enemies of the pope and the Roman Catholic Church – the most celebrated ones waged to counter Islamic power in the Holy Land and north Africa, but others an attack on Christians declared heretics in Europe. A key element of crusading wars was that the pope offered no less than God's forgiveness, the remission of past sins, and undying glory in God's kingdom, to those who took part.

FIRST CRUSADE AND CHRISTIAN TERRITORIES IN THE HOLY LAND

The First Crusade (1095-99) ended with the taking of Jerusalem in 1099 and led to the creation of four Christian territories in the Holy Land, known together as Outremer (from French for 'the land beyond the sea', and so called because the territories lay on the eastern shore of the Mediterranean). The County of Edessa (based on the city of Edessa, modern Urfa in Turkey) and the Principality of Antioch (based on the Syrian city of that name) were both formed in 1098. The Kingdom of Jerusalem was created in 1100 after the capture of the city, while the County of Tripoli was established in 1109.

SECOND AND THIRD CRUSADES

The First Crusade was followed by the Second (1147–49), called by Pope Eugenius III in response to the capture by

▲ *The Knights of St John defend the island of Rhodes against Ottoman attack in 1480.*

Muslim forces of Christian-held Edessa. Led by Louis VII of France and Conrad III of Germany, it ended dismally in a humiliating failure to take Damascus.

The Third Crusade (1187-92) was called by Pope Gregory VIII following the devastating defeat of the army of the Kingdom of Jerusalem by Muslim general Saladin at the Battle of the Horns of Hattin in July 1187 and Saladin's subsequent capture of Jerusalem. The crusade – led principally by King Philip II of France and King Richard I Coeur de Lion ('the Lion Hearted') of England – ended in a negotiated settlement without the hoped-for recapture of Jerusalem. There was a three-year truce and Christians were guaranteed access to Jerusalem as pilgrims.

FOURTH CRUSADE AND FAILURE

The Fourth Crusade began in 1202 and was a dismal failure. The initial aim was to attack the Holy Land by way of Egypt, in order to do this the crusade leaders negotiated with the great maritime power of Venice to provide a huge fleet of ships. They overreached themselves and were unable to pay for the ships. As a result the crusade fell under the control of Venice, Enrico Dandalo, and was diverted to attack an enemy of Venice, the Christian city of Zara (modern Zadar, Croatia).

Afterwards the crusade diverted a second time, to the Byzantine capital, Constantinople, and the crusaders besieged, captured and looted this great city. Then, with papal blessing, they abandoned the crusade and established a new government in Constantinople. Count Baldwin of Flanders was made emperor and a Venetian priest, Thomas Morosini, Patriarch of Constantinople.

FIFTH TO NINTH CRUSADES

The Fifth Crusade (1217–21) was called by Pope Innocent III in 1213. The crusaders, led by papal legate Pelagius, attacked Egypt to counter the power of the Ayyubid descendants of Saladin and succeeded in capturing the port of Damietta, but then made an unwise attempt to attack Cairo that ended in defeat by the Egyptian sultan al-Kamil, bringing a humiliating end to what had been a promising campaign.

A Sixth Crusade (1228–29) was led by Holy Roman Emperor Frederick II while he was excommunicated following a quarrel with the pope and was remarkably successful: through diplomacy rather than military might, he regained possession of Jerusalem, Nazareth and Bethlehem.

The Seventh Crusade (1248–54) was led by King Louis IX of France in response to the fall of Jerusalem to the Khwarezmian Turks in 1244. Once again attacking Egypt and capturing Damietta, it ended in humiliating failure. Louis was captured and ransomed at enormous cost, after which he travelled to Acre where he remained for some years.

The Eighth Crusade (1270) was again led by Louis IX. It set out for Syria but diverted to attack Tunis, where Louis died either of bubonic plague or dysentery and where the crusade came to nothing. The Ninth Crusade (1271–72) consisted of a campaign to the Holy Land led by the future King Edward I of England, in the course of which he made a few minor territorial gains – and famously survived an assassination attempt. Shortly afterwards, in 1291, the last European Christians in the Holy Land were driven out by another Muslim force, the Mamluks of Egypt, and Outremer was no more.

MONASTIC BROTHERHOODS

Military brotherhoods, first established around the time of the First Crusade, played a key role in defending the lands of Outremer. These included the Knights Hospitaller of St John of Jerusalem, the 'Poor Knights of Christ and the Temple of Solomon' (later better known as the Knights Templar), the Knights of Thomas of Canterbury at Acre and the Teutonic Knights, among others.

Many of these military monastic orders had long histories: the Knights Templar were charged with heresy and suppressed by the Catholic Church in the early 14th century, and most of their assets were passed to the Knights Hospitaller, who went on to win acclaim for their heroics in defending first Rhodes and then Malta against the Ottoman Turks in the 16th century. The warrior brotherhoods were an institution intimately connected with the crusading spirit and unique to the culture of chivalry.

CRUSADES IN EUROPE

Historians traditionally number the nine crusades listed above. There were also many crusades in Europe that do not make this list. Wars were fought against Islamic power in Spain and Portugal for 750 years from the 8th century, when Muslim Arabs and Berbers invaded from north Africa, to 1492 when the last Muslim territory in the peninsula, the city of Granada, was captured by the armies of Aragon and Castile. These wars were promoted as crusades from the 1090s.

Other major crusades in Europe included the Albigensian Crusade (1209-29) against the heretic Cathars or Albigensians of southern France, wars in the 12th–13th century against pagans in the Baltic region, as well as campaigns against heretic Hussites (followers of preacher Jan Hus) in Bohemia in 1420–32 and finally in Italy during the 12th–14th centuries against enemies of the papacy.

LEGACY AND AFTERMATH

The crusades played an important part in the long history of distrust between Christians and Muslims and contributed directly to the legacy of religious violence in the Holy Land. At the same time, however, they opened up contact between Europe and the East: Italian maritime republics such as Genoa and Venice grew rich in part form the trade that resulted and classical wisdom was brought to Europe from centres of learning in the Arab world. Both wealth and learning contributed to the Italian Renaissance while crusading ideology inspired the exploration of Africa and the Americas in the 15th and 16th centuries. The crusading movement's energy and religious devotion created a lasting legacy in the New World.

> **CRUSADE NUMBERING**
> Traditionally historians identified nine crusades but the labelling is arbitrary. There were not only a large number of other smaller crusades between the nine, but also many European crusades. Others were promoted as crusades with the grant of papal indulgences long after the year 1271 that marks the end of the Ninth Crusade. In the 18th century some historians counted eight crusades while some insisted there were just five (the First, Second, Third, Fifth and Seventh). Some modern historians also limit the numbered crusades to the first five from the traditional list, describing the rest by name. In this book, we follow the traditional numbering from the First to Ninth Crusades and refer to other campaigns by name (usually that of the destination or leader) and date.

▼ *Louis IX's ships on the Nile battle against the Saracens during the 7th Crusade.*

THE FOURTH, FIFTH AND SIXTH CRUSADES

In the first three decades of the 13th century, popes Innocent III (ruled 1198–1216), Honorius III (ruled 1216–27) and Gregory IX (ruled 1227–41) oversaw three major crusades to the East – the Fourth of 1202–04, the Fifth of 1217–21 and the Sixth of 1228. In his 18-year reign Innocent III also proclaimed a whole series of European crusades, including two against fellow Christians (the German lord Markward of Anweiler and the Albigensian heretics of southern France), one against Baltic pagans in northern Europe and one against the Muslim Almohad caliphs in Spain. In all of these encounters, Innocent and his successors worked with their utmost force to maintain papal control, for they saw crusading as a means to extend the power of Rome.

But the popes often failed to keep control of the powerful lords and complex alliances engaged in the crusades to the East. Of the three major Eastern crusades in these years, only the Fifth can be said to have remained under papal control through the office of papal legate Pelagius. It ended in abject failure, with the agreement of a humiliating peace treaty. Of the others, the Fourth slipped entirely from the papal control and ended up as little more than a pillaging expedition, while the Sixth ended as a seeming success, with Jerusalem in Christian hands and the position of Outremer bolstered. However, these successes had been achieved by the fiercely independent Frederick II of Germany working quite unilaterally to the papacy.

▲ *Venetian and French lords take stock after the sacking of Constantinople in 1204.*

◄ *The armies of the Fourth Crusade ignored an excommunication threat from Innocent III when they sacked the city of Zara in 1202.*

FIGHTING FOR VENICE

CRUSADERS DIVERT TO ATTACK ZARA

The newly elected Pope Innocent III called for another crusade to reclaim the Holy Land in August 1198. French barons responded to the call in 1201 and, choosing to travel by sea, negotiated with the doge of Venice, Enrico Dandolo, to transport them to the Holy Land. Failures of organization and recruitment resulted in them being in such severe debt to Venice that they had to agree to divert the crusaders to fight on the doge's behalf against the city of Zara, in Dalmatia (Croatia).

INNOCENT'S CALL TO ARMS

Pope Innocent's call to arms was largely directed at knights and noblemen rather than royalty. Like many others, Innocent believed that the Third Crusade had failed to liberate Jerusalem because it had been led by kings, and principally because of the inability of Richard I and Philip II to overcome their rivalries. This time the pope set out to establish the crusade as one strictly under papal control and nominated two legates, Soffredo of Pisa and Peter of Capuano, to be leaders 'humbly and religiously' of the crusade. Innocent

▼ *Venice rose to prominence as a centre for trade between western Europe and the rest of the known world – both the Byzantine Empire and Islamic territories beyond.*

later authorized the preaching of the crusade by a French priest named Fulk of Neuilly, a gifted orator.

The response to Innocent's call to arms was initially underwhelming, but then in November 1199 at a grand chivalric tournament at Ecry-sur-Aisne in Champagne, the 22-year-old host, Count Theobald of Champagne, and one of the leading competitors, the 27-year-old Count Louis of Blois, both took the cross after hearing a crusade sermon by Fulk of Neuilly. (Theobald was the younger brother of Henry of Champagne, then reigning as king of Jerusalem since he was the husband of Queen Isabella of Jerusalem, having married Isabella right after the assassination of her previous husband, Conrad of Montferrat.)

Theobald and Louis were followed by other noblemen, including Count Baldwin of Flanders and Simon of Montfort, 5th Earl of Leicester. (Simon was later captain general of French forces in the Albigensian Crusade and father of the Simon of Montfort who led baronial opposition to King Henry III of England and briefly ruled the country in the 1260s.) Also among the French noblemen who took the cross was Geoffrey of Villehardouin, who wrote an account of the crusade. Count Theobald was elected leader.

▲ *Earlier in his career, wily Venetian leader Enrico Dandolo had served his city as an ambassador to the Byzantine Empire. He knew the wealth of Constantinople.*

NEGOTIATIONS WITH VENICE

Theobald, Louis and Baldwin appointed six envoys to negotiate the necessary practical arrangements. The envoys approached Venice, the world's leading maritime power at the close of the 12th century, and commissioned a fleet to transport the crusader army to the Holy Land. They asked for sufficient ships to transport an army of 33,500 men – a wildly ambitious number, no less than seven times larger than the force taken by Philip II in 1190. The proposed army was to consist of 4,500 knights (with their horses), 9,000 squires and 20,000 infantry.

To supply a fleet to carry this army, plus nine months' supply of food and fodder, the Venetians demanded 85,000 marks; in addition they offered to provide 50 additional armed galleys 'for the love of God', on the condition that the city be granted one-half of any plunder that was seized by, either by land or sea. The deal was agreed, and consecrated in a lavish service in St Mark's, Venice.

The envoys' overambitious planning was to have severe consequences. The envoys also secretly agreed among themselves that the initial target for the crusade should be Egypt rather than Palestine. It had been proposed before, not least by Richard I during the Third Crusade, that the key to undermining Muslim strength in the Holy Land would be found in attacking Egypt. However, the revised target was kept secret because the majority of the knights and others who had taken the cross had done so with Jerusalem as their inspiration and goal.

A NEW LEADER

In May 1201, crusade leader Count Theobald died of a mysterious malady. He was replaced by the Italian count Boniface of Montferrat. In June 1202 crusaders began gathering in Venice. Only around 11,000 men had arrived by October, partly because some had sailed directly from ports in southern France; the original target of 33,500 had been far too ambitious. The fleet of ships was ready – but the crusaders could not pay for it in full. After a prolonged stalemate, the Venetian doge offered to postpone full

▼ *Pope Innocent III felt the church had to strengthen its position against heretics within the Christian church.*

▲ *Baldwin of Flanders played a leading role in the Fourth Crusade from start to shameful finish. He was made emperor of the Latin Empire of Constantinople.*

payment of the shortfall until the crusaders were able to raise the money through looting, but only if the crusaders came to the aid of Venice by reconquering its former colony of Zara in Hungary (modern Zadar in Croatia). This was a Christian city, under the protection of the Roman Catholic king, Emeric of Hungary, who had himself taken the cross.

The crusaders effectively had no choice. The doge, Enrico Dandolo, elected to take the cross and sail with them – despite being in his 80s and virtually blind. He was an extremely capable and intelligent man, and remarkable healthy for his age.

THE ATTACK ON ZARA

The crusade fleet sailed in November 1202, bound for Zara. The papal legate Peter Capuano approved the deal as the only way to prevent the crusade foundering altogether, but Pope Innocent III wrote a letter threatening the crusade leaders with excommunication if they attacked fellow Christians. The citizens of Zara hung banners emblazoned with the cross from their windows and on the city walls in the hope of forestalling the assault. But the attack went ahead.

After a siege of five days, Zara surrendered to the crusade leaders, and accepted Venice's claim of suzerainty. The victorious army entered the city and systematically looted it. They then decided to spend the winter there before proceeding with the crusade.

ON TO CONSTANTINOPLE

CRUSADERS AGREE TO RESTORE DEPOSED EMPEROR TO THRONE

After the sacking of Zara, the crusaders took another unexpected diversion. Exiled Byzantine prince Alexius Angelus offered their leaders astonishing levels of funding and military support for the remainder of the expedition if they agreed first to sail to Constantinople and depose the emperor, Alexius III.

BYZANTINE NEGOTIATIONS

Emperor Isaac II Angelus had in 1195 been blinded, deposed and imprisoned by his own brother, who took the throne as Emperor Alexius III. The deposed emperor's son, Prince Alexius Angelus, had escaped into exile and was seeking support to restore his father to the throne. In the winter of 1202 he was a guest of Philip of Swabia, who was his brother-in-law, having married Alexius's sister Irene in May 1197.

At Philip's court, Alexius met Boniface of Montferrat, the elected leader of the Fourth Crusade, who had left his fellow crusaders in Venice before they embarked to make the attack on Zara. (Philip was the youngest son of Emperor Frederick I Barbarossa and was king of Germany; he had been elected Holy Roman emperor in 1198 following the death of Henry VI, but

Pope Innocent opposed his succession, preferring the rival claim of Otto, son of Henry the Lion, Duke of Saxony. Boniface was one of Philip's leading feudal vassals.)

Prince Alexius made a remarkable offer to Boniface: if the crusaders diverted the expedition to Constantinople in order forcibly to right the wrongs brought about by the usurper emperor Alexius III, he would provide 200,000 silver marks to meet the army's current expenses, supply food for the entire force, send 10,000 men and 20 galleys to support the planned crusading expedition against Egypt for an entire year, establish a permanent force of 500 Byzantine knights in the Holy Land – and put the Greek Orthodox Church under the authority of the pope in Rome.

Boniface of Montferrat returned to the crusaders, with Prince Alexius in his party, and news of his very generous offer. The main leaders agreed to the plan, arguing that this diversion was the only way to bring about the crusade's ultimate aims, but it was far from universally popular. Several noblemen, including the French knight Simon of Montfort, withdrew in disgust; when news of the decision reached Rome, Pope Innocent sent letters forbidding an attack on Constantinople.

However, these letters arrived after the main body of the crusade set sail for Constantinople on Easter Monday 1203, too late; in any case, the crusaders had so many reasons to move against the Byzantines that it is doubtful whether or not the letters would have had any effect.

REASONS TO ATTACK THE BYZANTINE EMPIRE

Venice had a longstanding quarrel with the Byzantine emperor, dating back to the 1170s, when Emperor Manuel I Comnenus had arrested Venetian merchants and confiscated their valuable goods. Moreover, the current usurper emperor, Alexius III, was granting preferable trading terms to Venice's rivals, Genoa and Pisa.

Boniface of Montferrat also had a quarrel with the Byzantine Empire. His younger brother Rainier had in 1179 married Maria Comnena, daughter of Emperor Manuel I Comnenus, and had been given the title 'Caesar'. Both Rainier and Maria had then been killed by poison in Constantinople in 1182 and Boniface claimed that Byzantine territory that he believed had been given to Rainier was now rightfully his.

Another important factor, although not one that can have been discussed openly, was that launching the planned attack on Egypt was not in the interests of the Venetians, who had a trading colony in Alexandria; according to some interpretations of contemporary documents, the Venetians may have secretly made a treaty in 1202 with Saladin's brother al-Adil, in power in Egypt, to divert a crusading attack away from Egypt in return for improved trading privileges there.

◀ *Zara surrenders to Venetian control. Venice had twice invaded Zara in the 12th century before the opportunity arose to impose its will on the city.*

▲ *After spurning orders from Pope Alexius III to move on to Jerusalem, the huge Venetian fleet of over 200 ships, attacked the great walls of Constantinople.*

On top of these considerations, relations had been extremely strained between the 'Latins' in the European crusader army and the 'Greeks' of the Byzantine Empire, from the time of the First Crusade.

But probably most pressing of all reasons was that the crusaders in Zara did not manage to raise enough money in looting the city to pay off their debt to the city of Venice. They needed to generate wealth, and the diversion to Constantinople, although officially being launched to restore the deposed emperor, also raised the tantalizing prospect of looting the imperial capital.

ARRIVAL AT CONSTANTINOPLE

The vast crusade fleet, consisting of 60 war galleys as well as 50 large transports and 100 horse transports, arrived at Constantinople on St John the Baptist's Day, 24 June 1203. The ships did not land before the city, but sailed on to capture and install themselves in Chalcedon and Chrysopolis on the other side of the Bosphorus.

There they were visited by an envoy from Emperor Alexius III declaring that he would provide money and supplies if they moved swiftly on towards Jerusalem, but they sent back the reply that they did not recognize his authority and that the lands he ruled belonged to his nephew who was in the crusader camp. Then the crusaders sent young Alexius to the city with ten galleys of soldiers, to ask the

inhabitants of the city, who were arrayed on its walls, whether they would recognize the rule of the deposed Isaac II Angelus and his son. They replied that they did not know these names, and jeered at the soldiers.

On 5 July – to the sound of trumpets, tabors and kettledrums – the full might of the crusader army embarked on to transports to cross the Bosphorus and begin the siege of the city. According to the eyewitness account of a crusader knight from Picardy, named Robert of Clari, the people of Constantinople armed themselves and climbed on the roofs of their houses and up the many towers of the city. They saw the vast fleet. 'It seemed to them,' Robert wrote, 'that the ocean and the land were shaking, and that the wide waves were covered over entirely with ships.'

THE SACK OF CONSTANTINOPLE
RAPE, MURDER AND LOOTING AS CRUSADERS SHAME THE CROSS

The Fourth Crusade's diversion to Constantinople, officially performed to restore the deposed Emperor Isaac II Angelus to the imperial throne, degenerated into a full-scale attack on the city, followed by three lawless days of rampant looting. The greed-driven ransacking of this historic Christian city must rival the savage slaughter of the inhabitants of Jerusalem in 1099 as the nadir of the entire crusading era.

THE FIRST SIEGE OF CONSTANTINOPLE

When the crusaders crossed the Bosphorus to attack Constantinople on 5 July 1203, the usurper emperor Alexius III led his army to the Bosphorus shore to fight, but such was the intimidating might of the crusader and Venetian fleets that the Byzantine troops fled before the crusaders landed. The knights had embarked on their transports already mounted on horseback and now were able to gallop right off the ships, along platforms lowered on to the beach. They chased the terrified Greeks as far as the city walls.

The crusaders settled in for a siege that lasted until 17 July. On that day, they launched a two-pronged attack by land and sea. The Venetians captured the Tower of Galata on the northern side of the Golden Horn, which allowed them to break the protective chain that stretched across the harbour preventing ships sailing in. The fleet then passed easily into the harbour. The aged doge of Venice rode in the foremost Venetian ship, with the city banner of St Mark before him, urging his men on, and then clambered on to land and planted the banner in the soil.

▼ *Piety was nowhere to be found as the crusaders ran amok in the historic city of Constantinople, looting, drinking, raping and wrecking treasures they could not carry.*

RESTORATION OF ISAAC II

The usurper Alexius III fled, with as many jewels and as much imperial treasure as he could take from the treasury. The Greeks of Constantinople then took former emperor Isaac II, blind and bewildered after so many years in prison, and restored him to the throne, hoping to pre-empt any actions by the Venetians. But the invaders needed Alexius to be in power, so he could make good his lavish promises to them. They engineered his election as co-emperor alongside his father. Isaac II and Alexius IV were so crowned on 1 August 1203 in the Church of Hagia Sophia.

With the treasury severely depleted, however, Alexius IV was unable to honour the promises made in Zara. He asked the crusaders to extend their stay for six more months to help him consolidate his position on the throne and to raise money from his subjects.

REVOLT OF ALEXIUS DOUKAS

The crusaders and Venetians agreed reluctantly for they could not afford to leave without Alexius's finance. They camped outside the city, but often ventured into it to seek entertainment, on one occasion starting a fire that raged for an entire week. The people of Constantinople grew restless, and rebelled against their joint emperors in January 1204: Isaac and Alexius barricaded themselves in the palace, sending a courtier named Alexius Doukas or Murtzuphlus to seek help from the crusaders. But Murtzuphlus – who was a popular figure, having taken part in number of skirmishes against the crusaders – seized his opportunity: he deposed the emperors and took the crown for himself, to great popular acclaim. He took power as Alexius V, strangling Alexius IV; the weak and aged Isaac II died in prison a few days later, probably of natural causes.

▲ Baldwin of Flanders is elected emperor in Constantinople on 16 May, 1204.

THE SECOND SIEGE OF CONSTANTINOPLE

Now the crusaders and Venetians had no chance of receiving the wealth and military help they had been promised. They determined to take the city by force. The pope declared that Christians could be attacked if they were actively preventing the furtherance of the crusade – and it was possible to argue that the people of Constantinople had done this by deposing the emperor who had promised to help in the holy war.

The besieging army agreed that six Venetians and six crusaders would form an electoral college to elect a new emperor, who would have a quarter of the empire. The other three-quarters would be split between Venice and the crusaders. The crusade's clergymen came up with justifications for the attack, suggesting that the people of Constantinople deserved to be punished for committing the mortal sin of murdering their anointed emperor, and

that in any case they should be forcibly brought into the Roman Catholic Church. They declared, moreover, that knights and soldiers who died in the attack would benefit from the indulgence granted by the pope as if they had carried the crusade to its conclusion.

THE CITY IS SACKED

The Venetians and crusaders embarked on a second siege of Constantinople on 6 April and took the city just seven days later, on 13 April. Emperor Alexius V fled; the crusader leaders and the doge of Venice installed themselves in his abandoned palace. The army was allowed three days of looting.

They went on the rampage, committing murder and rape, stealing indiscriminately, ransacking churches, destroying ancient objects of art, and taking sacred relics. Drunken soldiers were joined in the looting by knights, noblemen, priests and bishops. According to Geoffrey of Villehardouin, more booty was seized in the sacking of Constantinople than ever before in the entire history of the world.

THE LATIN EMPIRE OF CONSTANTINOPLE

In the aftermath, the papal legate absolved the crusaders of their vow to carry the expedition on to the Holy Land. The crusaders and Venetians set about creating a new government in Constantinople. Count Baldwin of Flanders was elected emperor and crowned in the Church of Hagia Sophia on 16 May 1204 by the papal legate. Baldwin declared himself a vassal of the Pope, and received the recognition of Rome. Thomas Morosini, a priest from Venice, was appointed the first Latin Patriarch of Constantinople. European-style feudalism was introduced, with 600 knights being granted fiefdoms.

Boniface of Montferrat had probably expected to be elected emperor himself, but he had to make do with a kingdom formed from Byzantine territory and based on Salonica (modern Thessaloniki). The doge stayed on in Constantinople overseeing Venetian interests. He died there in 1205, aged 97, and was buried in the Church of Hagia Sophia.

▼ The bronze horses seized from the Hippodrome were sent back to Venice and erected in St Mark's Square. They are visible within the cupola of this plan.

A NEW VIEW OF CRUSADING
CRUSADING REFORMS AND INNOVATIONS OF POPE INNOCENT III

Pope Innocent III, who reigned for 18 years from 1198 to 1216, established crusading on a new footing. He preached two holy wars in the East and proclaimed crusades against pagan Europeans, heretic Christians and political enemies as well against Muslims. In every single year of his rule, a crusade was being fought somewhere in the world, officially in his name.

PAPAL POWER

Educated in Rome, Paris and Bologna, Lothar dei Conti di Segni was elected Pope Innocent III at the age of just 37 on 8 January 1198. He had a brilliant mind, a rare gift for canon law, and a powerful desire to build on the Church reforms of Pope Gregory VII and establish the papacy as the pre-eminent religious and political force. Almost at once he set about promoting a crusade to the Holy Land. He also began negotiations with the Byzantine emperor to unite the Eastern and Western churches under papal control in Rome.

This plan was ruined when in 1202–04 the Fourth Crusade spiralled out of his control, with the army effectively serving the aged doge of Venice and diverting to Zara in Hungary and then to an attack on

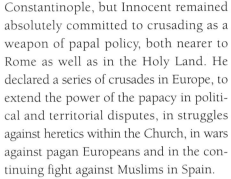

▲ *Pope Innocent III, like his predecessors, proclaimed various crusades, but uniquely he sanctioned military campaigns against non-Muslim powers and heretic Christians.*

▼ *In 1209 Innocent III gave St Francis of Assisi permission to found a religious order. Francis was loyal to church and clergy and Innocent may have wanted to utilize his itinerant monks to counter heresy.*

Constantinople, but Innocent remained absolutely committed to crusading as a weapon of papal policy, both nearer to Rome as well as in the Holy Land. He declared a series of crusades in Europe, to extend the power of the papacy in political and territorial disputes, in struggles against heretics within the Church, in wars against pagan Europeans and in the continuing fight against Muslims in Spain.

Already in 1199 he had declared a crusade against Markward of Anweiler, a follower of the recently deceased Holy Roman Emperor Henry VI, who had come into direct conflict with papal policy in southern Italy and Sicily: Innocent declared Markward 'another Saladin', an enemy of Christianity who was attempting to undermine the Fourth Crusade; he promised those who fought Markward the same indulgences available to those who travelled to the Holy Land.

In 1204 Innocent launched a crusade against pagans in the Baltic region of northern Europe: in a letter to the archbishop of Bremen he offered the same indulgence available for a Holy Land crusade to those who attempted to convert Baltic pagans by force. Then, in 1208, he called a crusade against the Albigensians, a group of heretical Christians in southern France, and again promised those who fought in his service the same indulgences available for a Holy Land crusade. In this case, the indulgence would be granted in return for just 40 days of military service.

In 1212 he proclaimed a crusade in Spain against the Muslim Almohad caliphs, and that year crusader knights and infantrymen from southern France and Spain, fighting alongside the armies of Sancho VII of Navarre, Peter II of Aragon and Alfonso VIII of Castile, won a resounding victory over a Muslim army at the Battle of Las Navas de Tolosa. This was a crucial Christian victory in the centuries-long struggle against Muslims in Spain.

The following year, in 1213, Innocent began to organize the Fifth Crusade to the Holy Land and he died in 1216, while preaching the crusade in Perugia. In addition to promoting crusading in so many guises, Innocent also made a number of changes and clarifications in the financing and organization of these holy wars.

CRUSADING TAXES

Seeing that the cost of crusading put off many potential holy warriors/soldiers of Christ, Innocent set out to establish a secure financial basis for the crusading movement. In promoting the Fourth Crusade in 1199 he imposed a tax on clerical incomes – one-fortieth of their annual revenue for one year – to raise money for the expedition. He said that this would not set a precedent, but in fact it did – and clerical taxes were subsequently imposed in 1215 for the Fifth Crusade (one-twentieth of revenue for three years), in 1245, after Jerusalem had fallen to the Khwarismian Turks (another tax of one-twentieth for three years), and again in 1263 and 1274.

Innocent made a major innovation in 1213, while promoting the Fifth Crusade, when he ruled that crusade vows could be redeemed by payment of money. This meant that those Christians who could not take the cross because of age, infirmity, physical weakness or lack of equipment could pay for others to go on their behalf – and have a part in the spiritual benefit of the crusade without leaving home.

Innocent also sought to improve the arrangements for the promotion of crusades, introducing new procedures and appointments for preaching the cross. For the Fourth Crusade, he despatched Cistercian monks to give crusade sermons, while for the Fifth Crusade he sent out a group of trained reformers to promote the expedition. Innocent even set out to boost attendance at crusade sermons by offering a 'partial indulgence' (the cancellation of part of a penance due) simply for listening to a preacher's attempts to convince people to take the cross.

CRUSADER PRIVILEGES

Pope Innocent also codified and clarified the privileges available to crusaders, notably in the appendix *Ad liberandum* to the decrees of the Fourth Lateran Council of 1215. The most important was the indulgence. Previous indulgences had been given on the understanding that – by the pope's authority – God would view the crusader's sufferings on crusade as 'satisfactory', meaning that they cancelled debts due for previous sins. This sparked debate among canon lawyers as to whether any penance could be satisfactory in this way. Under Innocent III, the indulgence guaranteed a crusader that all punishment for previous sins would be remitted (both in this world and the next) whether or not as a penance it proved to be satisfactory in God's eyes; the guarantee was given on God's behalf by the pope. Other notable privileges included: a crusader's property and dependents would be protected by the Church; a crusader would be freed of the obligation to settle debts or pay interest on them while away on crusade; he would also be exempted from feudal service, taxes and tolls for the duration of the crusade; a crusader would have the right to hospitality from the Church while on crusade; anyone who had been excommunicated would be freed from his punishment by taking the cross, and while on crusade could interact with excommunicated Christians without fear of punishment; and a crusader could take a crusade vow in place of another vow or instead of returning stolen goods.

▼ *Innocent sent a monk named Dominic to dispute with the Albigensians. In a trial by fire, Dominic's books were miraculously saved from the flames while others burned. But Dominic could not persuade them.*

THE CHILDREN'S CRUSADES
SPONTANEOUS OUTBURSTS OF ENTHUSIASM FOR HOLY WAR

According to chronicle accounts, in 1212 thousands of poor children were inspired by charismatic preachers to leave their homes in France and Germany to travel to Jerusalem on crusade and save the holy places there. This was not a holy war: none of these crusaders envisaged using force, for they believed that through faith the power of God would be enough to achieve their purpose.

FROM FRANCE AND GERMANY
There were two waves to the Children's Crusade, one issuing from northern France and one beginning in Germany. The story goes that in May 1212 a shepherd boy named Stephen from Cloyes-sur-le-Loir (near Châteaudun in the Vermandois) walked to see King Philip at Saint-Denis and reported that he had had a vision of Christ instructing him to lead a crusade to Jerusalem. Philip attempted to send the boy home, but Stephen embarked on a preaching tour of the countryside and gathered many followers among the youth and children of the area.

▼ *Christ Pantocrator (Ruler of all). Both German and French Children's Crusades were called in His name.*

He promised them that because Christ had called the crusade, He would supply food and water on the march and bring them safely to the Holy Land, and that if they followed Stephen to the south of France they would find that Christ would part the waters of the Mediterranean to enable them to walk all the way.

Around the same time, a German youth named Nicholas of Cologne mobilized a similar pilgrim army in the Rhineland. He called for the liberation of the Holy Sepulchre and, like Stephen, promised that the seas would be parted by God as they made their way to the Holy Land, demonstrating their faith by trusting in His deliverance. Stephen's followers were mainly children and youths, although there were also adults and priests in the company. People of both sexes joined up – according to the contemporary Annals of Marbach, as the crusaders marched through the countryside young people simply downed tools in the fields or abandoned the flocks they were minding and joined the march.

THE FRENCH MARCH SOUTH
The French group headed southwards towards the Mediterranean coast under Stephen's leadership. The group contained principally children and young people, mostly under the age of 15, both from very poor and more prosperous backgrounds; there were also a few priests and other adults in Stephen's following. Many died of exhaustion, illness or starvation on the way, and others simply drifted away, but when they reached Marseilles they were still as many as 30,000 in number.

The waters did not part as promised. Some pilgrims became disillusioned and wandered off, but many waited on, believing that God would still deliver them. Finally two merchants from the city, named Hugh Ferreus (Iron Hugh) and William Porcus (Pig William), offered to

▲ *Following in the footsteps of the Tafurs (the pious peasants who accompanied the First Crusade) the participants in the Children's Crusades are said to have believed that their faith would be enough to bring success.*

carry them by ship to the Holy Land and Stephen embarked with the still sizeable remnant of his following in seven ships. They were never seen again in France, but later reports (supposedly based on an eye-witness account by a survivor of the expedition) revealed that after two ships were lost in a storm near Sardinia the other merchants sailed to Bougie and Alexandria in northern Africa, where they sold the surviving children into slavery among the Saracens.

THE GERMAN CHILDREN'S CRUSADE
Meanwhile, the German contingent made its way across the Alps into northern Italy and proceeded to Genoa. Some participants settled in Genoa, others went on to Pisa and some made it all the way to Rome, where they had an audience with Innocent III. Innocent told them to return home, but to that they should preserve

pueri (Latin for 'boys') in some accounts, and this was misinterpreted by later chroniclers as a movement of children when in fact it was a migration of adults. Moreover, the largely secular movements of the poor seeking food and work were cast as pilgrimages, and even crusades, under the influence of the thriving popular cult of the Innocents. These were the children who were slaughtered, according to the Gospel of St Matthew, on the orders of King Herod, in response to a prophecy that a newborn 'King of the Jews' was destined to seize his throne. The Innocents were celebrated as the first Christian martyrs as part of a celebration of poverty and simple piety, which was also fed by memories of the poor but ferociously pious Tafurs of the First Crusade, and it may be that in the light of this cult the mass migrations of country poor were reimagined as a crusade of the Innocents.

▲ Philip II travelled on the Third Crusade but afterwards was not interested in crusading. He did not help Innocent III in his holy war against Albigensians in southern France.

their enthusiasm for crusading and put it to use in adulthood. From Pisa, two shiploads of German children embarked but were never heard of again.

A POPULAR LEGEND?

Some modern historians suggest that these accounts may be largely popular legends based on memories of the mass movement of country poor in the early 13th century. According to this theory, the poor forced into wandering by poverty were called

THE PIED PIPER OF HAMELIN

According to some historians, the German folktale of the Pied Piper of Hamelin has its origins in the events of the Children's Crusade. In the folktale, the people of the German town of Hamelin were plagued by rats, and accepted the offer of a vagrant in colourful clothes that he would clear the town of vermin for a fixed sum; he played a marvellous tune on his pipe and the rats followed him out of the town to the river, where they drowned. The people of Hamelin then refused to pay up the agreed fee, and so the piper returned when the folk were all in church and, playing his pipe once more, led all the town's children away. They were never seen again. The first known appearance of the piper of Hamelin is in a church window in Hamelin dated to c.1300, but this window – now destroyed – simply showed the piper leading away several children dressed in white; the rats were not added to the story until the late 1500s. Another theory is that the folktale is based on memories of the 13th-century migration of people to settle in eastern Europe.

▼ The Pied Piper leads the children of the village of Hamelin on their merry dance of no return. Was he based on a folk memory of the preachers who led off the young on the Children's Crusades?

THE FIFTH CRUSADE
CRUSADERS HUMILIATED IN EGYPT

In April 1213 Innocent III proclaimed another crusade to the Holy Land in the papal bull *Quia major*. The pope was determined to bring about the recovery of the Holy Sepulchre in Jerusalem as a symbol of papal supremacy throughout Christendom. In the event, the crusade fleet sailed to Egypt, where after taking the port of Damietta they marched to a humiliating defeat at the hands of Saladin's nephew, Sultan al-Kamil.

The crusade was promoted enthusiastically by travelling preachers, and regular processions. Innocent made the call again at the fourth Lateran Council of 1215; the departure date for the new crusade was set for 1217. Innocent died in May 1216, and his successor Pope Honorius III took over the organization of the expedition.

THE FIRST WAVE OF CRUSADERS
The first armies to depart were led by Duke Leopold VI of Austria and King Andrew II of Hungary, in 1217. They sailed to Acre, and mobilized with John of Brienne, King of Jerusalem, Prince Bohemond IV of Antioch and King Hugh I of Cyprus to fight Ayyubid descendants of Saladin in Syria – principally the great general's brother al-Adil, who had succeeded him as sultan. Very little was achieved on this expedition, although a number of sacred relics were captured. In January 1218 King Andrew headed home by way of Constantinople.

THE SIEGE OF DAMIETTA
In 1218 a contingent of German crusaders arrived in Acre. Now the target was switched to Ayyubid possessions in Egypt. In May 1218 German troops under the command of John of Brienne sailed to Egypt and besieged the port of Damietta. Their plan was to take this city as a supply base before moving on to attack Cairo.

On 25 August they captured the tower just outside Damietta, but did not push

▲ *Francis of Assisi attempts to convince al-Kamil of the merits of Christianity during the meeting he was granted with the sultan.*

on and take the city itself, preferring to wait for reinforcements – for news had reached them that a French and English army was sailing from Genoa while the Spanish cardinal Pelagius of Albano had embarked from Brindisi.

Pelagius arrived in mid-September, but struggled to impose his authority, for he was not a military man and the assembled army looked to John of Brienne as its leader. German soldiers also had another claim on their loyalty: they were expecting the arrival of Frederick II, who had taken the cross as early as 1215, but had since focused his energies on consolidating his position in Germany and Italy.

In October the English and French arrived: still the crusaders, hampered by lack of leadership and a badly organized siege, did not take the city. Their camp was flooded following storms in November and December and hit by an epidemic in which as many as 10 per cent of their number died – including English cardinal Robert of Courçon, one of the principal crusade preachers.

OFFER OF PEACE
By this time, al-Adil had died and his son al-Kamil had taken his position as sultan. In spring 1219, judging it inevitable that the crusaders would take Damietta, Sultan al-Kamil made overtures of peace – if the crusaders agreed to lift the siege of Damietta and leave Egypt, he promised to give them possession of Jerusalem, and the entire Kingdom as it had been before the Battle of the Horns of Hattin, and also to return the relic of the True Cross – which had been in Muslim hands ever since that battle. All he wanted to retain was the fortresses of Oultrejordain and the territory they controlled, so that the two main parts of his empire, Egypt and Syria, could maintain contact – for this territory he would pay tribute of 30,000 bezants. In the Holy Land, al-Kamil's brother al-Mu'azzam, the ruler of Syria, dismantled the fortifications of Jerusalem so that the Christians would not be able to defend it.

King John of Jerusalem and the barons of his kingdom urged acceptance. So did the crusader knights of Germany, France and England, for it seemed to them that the offer delivered the prize for which the crusade had been mobilized. But Pelagius made the judgement that the Holy City could not be bartered for and that the Christian army should not negotiate with the infidel. He had the support of the knights of the military orders, who were unhappy at the proposed loss of their treasured castles of Krak and Montreal in Oultrejordain, and of the Italians, who were determined to capture Damietta in order to establish a trading position there.

A SAINTLY VISITOR
The siege continued. In August or September, the saintly monk Francis of Assisi arrived in order to argue for non-violence. He had an audience with al-Kamil and so impressed the sultan that he was allowed to preach to his subjects.

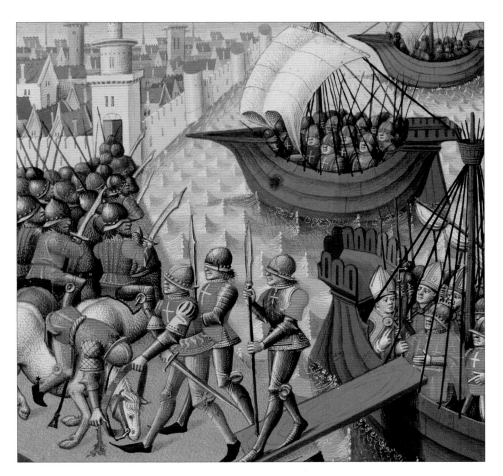

and waiting, Pelagius and the crusade leaders suddenly became decisive – and ordered a march up the river Nile towards Cairo, with the idea of making the manoeuvre before the beginning of the river's annual floods.

DEFEAT IN THE MUD

The sultan brought his troops out to meet the crusade army and the advance was stalled. Then the river began to rise and the crusaders became cut off from their supply ships by Egyptian vessels.

Pelagius saw that the campaign had gone badly wrong and ordered a retreat, but Sultan al-Kamil destroyed flood control barriers and the waters swept in, stranding the crusader troops in the thick Nile mud. When Al-Kamil launched a night attack, the crusade army suffered very heavy losses and Pelagius had to negotiate a humiliating peace treaty under which the crusaders evacuated Damietta, agreed an eight-year truce and left Egypt. All they had in return was a promise that the piece of the True Cross would be handed over – but when it came to it, the Muslims could not find this most sacred of Christian relics.

A STRONG POSITION LOST

Finally in November 1219 the crusaders captured Damietta and, true to form, sacked and looted the city. Had they marched swiftly south against Cairo they would probably have ended the rule of Sultan al-Kamil and made Egypt a Christian country. Instead they became embroiled in a quarrel over who had the right to claim Damietta, with John of Brienne declaring the town to be his possession and legate Pelagius claiming it on behalf of Rome.

The army was still expecting the imminent arrival of Emperor Frederick II, and for no less than 20 months the crusaders sat in Damietta. From Rome came official confirmation of Pelagius as commander-in-chief of the crusading army. John of Brienne returned to Acre.

In June 1221 Sultan al-Kamil made a fresh peace offer, on largely the same terms as before. Again Pelagius refused. Finally in July, Emperor Frederick's advance party arrived under the command of Duke

▲ *Crusader troops land prior to launching an assault on the port of Damietta.*

Louis I of Bavaria – the emperor himself sent orders to await his arrival. John of Brienne returned from Acre. But then, after more than 18 months of indecision

▼ *The crusaders suffered a heavy defeat as they tried to retreat following their ill-judged advance up the river Nile.*

JERUSALEM REGAINED

THE SIXTH CRUSADE OF 1228–29

The Sixth Crusade was led by Holy Roman Emperor Frederick II. Without even engaging the army of Ayyubid sultan al-Kamil in battle, he negotiated the return of Jerusalem (as well as Nazareth, Jaffa, Sidon and Bethlehem) to Christian control, although under the terms of the agreement the Temple Mount area of Jerusalem, which includes the Dome of the Rock and the al-Aqsa mosque, was to remain in Muslim hands.

KING OF GERMANY TAKES THE CROSS

Frederick II was crowned King of Germany in 1215, and in that year first took the cross as a young man of just 19 in response to the April 1213 call to arms made by Pope Innocent III. As we have seen, he was repeatedly said to be preparing to embark to take part in the disastrous Fifth Crusade to Egypt, and even sent an advance party of his force in 1221. It is probable that had he gone in

▼ Frederick II Stupor Mundi – 'the wonder of the world' – was his own master and kept the Sixth Crusade free of papal control.

person to Egypt he would have been able to oust the papal prelate Pelagius from control of the army and under more effective leadership the crusaders might have taken Cairo and defeated Sultan al-Kamil – and the crusade would have ended in triumph rather than disaster. However, he was embroiled in consolidating his position in Germany and Italy and did not go.

HOLY ROMAN EMPEROR – AND KING OF JERUSALEM

In 1220, before the end of the Fifth Crusade, Frederick was crowned Holy Roman Emperor by Pope Honorius III on 22 November 1220. At this point he renewed his promise to go on crusade, but it was to be 1228 before he finally arrived in the Holy Land.

By the time he did so he was notionally king of Jerusalem, for in 1225 he had married Isabella (or Yolande), Queen of Jerusalem. Isabella was the daughter of Maria of Montferrat, the previous Queen of Jerusalem, and of King John of Brienne, who had ruled as King of Jerusalem on account of his marriage to Maria. Isabella had become Queen of Jerusalem as an infant on the death of her mother in 1212. In 1225 Frederick married her in a magnificent ceremony at Brindisi Cathedral, then despatched a message to John of Brienne, who was already in his late 70s, that as a result of the marriage the Holy Roman Emperor was now also King of Jerusalem.

STUPOR MUNDI

The grandson of Frederick I Barbarossa, Frederick II was an extraordinary figure, known to his contemporaries as *Stupor Mundi*, 'Wonder of the World'. He was fluent in six languages – German, Italian, French, Greek, Latin and Arabic; he was a mathematician and philosopher and a great patron of the arts. He was worldly, ferociously intelligent and scathing of

▲ Frederick was twice crowned king, in 1212 and 1215, before he was crowned Holy Roman Emperor in Rome in 1220.

religion – he reportedly declared that 'Moses, Christ and Muhammad were all imposters' and intimated that the pope had been found on a dunghill. At Palermo he kept a harem in the style of Oriental rulers – and to this he despatched his young bride immediately after the wedding. This was not a man who could easily be forced to become a papal agent.

CONFLICT WITH THE PAPACY

A key reason for Frederick's repeated delaying of his crusade was that he was embroiled in a long-running struggle with Rome, both over lands in Italy and over the centuries-old issue of whether pope or Holy Roman emperor was the rightful leader of Christendom. When he first took the cross in 1215, the then pope, Innocent III, wanted to stop him going – he was determined to maintain control of the crusade and wanted to avoid the involvement of so powerful and independent a man as Frederick. Subsequent popes, however, were willing to countenance his involvement in the holy war as they believed he would bring success. Moreover, when he finally departed for the Holy Land the territories in Italy would be left unprotected.

Frederick embarked for the Holy Land in 1227, but an epidemic struck his fleet and he himself was laid low with fever, so

▲ *Gregory IX was nephew to Pope Innocent III and also attempted to maintain a strong papal authority. Frederick defied him.*

the crusaders returned to Italy. The new pope, Gregory IX, excommunicated him for breaking his crusader vows.

AN ALLIANCE WITH EGYPT

In Italy, Frederick received a diplomatic mission at Palermo from Sultan al-Kamil seeking military help against his own brother, al-Mu'azzam, and offering Jerusalem as a reward. This played right into Frederick's hands – all along he had wanted to lead a crusade on his own terms, not as an instrument of papal power but as emperor, secular ruler of Christendom. Despite the excommunication, which technically meant that he could not lead a crusade, he finally embarked. Pope Gregory issued a ringing condemnation of the emperor's actions.

He sailed via Cyprus, where he quarrelled with the regent John of Ibelin, lord of Beirut and Arsuf. Frederick imposed rule in his name by a group of five local knights (*baillis*) and then sailed for Acre, the capital of the Kingdom of Jerusalem.

SUCCESS IN THE HOLY LAND

On arrival, Frederick did not receive undivided support: he had alienated the important Ibelin group, and the Church hierarchy led by Patriarch Gerald of Lausanne followed the leadership of the

pope by being hostile. His only supporters were the barons of the Kingdom, the Teutonic knights and the German army.

Sultan al-Kamil in fact no longer needed Frederick's support, for al-Mu'azzam had died. But after Frederick made a show of force by marching down the Mediterranean coast from Acre to Jaffa with a crusader army of around 3,000, al-Kamil agreed to honour the proposed deal and Jerusalem was returned to Latin control in a treaty signed on 18 February 1229. The treaty also established a ten-year truce and guaranteed Muslims free access to Jerusalem to visit their shrines on the Temple Mount; as well as Nazareth and Bethlehem, the Christians received a corridor of land linking Jerusalem to Acre.

TRIUMPH IN JERUSALEM

Frederick marched into Jerusalem on 17 March 1229. He took part in a crowning of sorts the following day, and proclaimed himself Lord of Jerusalem. It was not a formal coronation because the Patriarch was still opposed to these events, and had remained in Acre – in fact, Frederick lifted the crown on to his own head and, according to some, used the imperial crown, not that of Jerusalem.

The treaty was generally highly unpopular on both sides. The Muslims felt cheated by their sultan – the imams in

Egypt and Damascus proclaimed a period of public mourning because Islam had been betrayed. The Christian knights felt that the treaty was far less favourable than the terms offered and turned down at Damietta. Moreover, as Pelagius and their predecessors had argued, they felt that the Kingdom of Jerusalem should have been won back by the sword and not through negotiation. The Latin settlers argued that the narrow corridor of land between Acre and Jerusalem was impracticable since it could not be adequately defended. In spite of this dissent, the fact remains that Frederick had achieved the crusade's ultimate aim by putting the Holy City back in Christian hands.

Frederick left Jerusalem in May and returned to Italy. He had to drive out papal troops commanded by John of Brienne, which had invaded his Italian territories. Later in the year the pope, humbled by defeat in battle, lifted the excommunication. But the struggle between pope and emperor was far from over – and a decade later, Frederick not only found himself excommunicated a second time, but also had a crusade declared against his territorial holdings in Italy.

▼ *At Frederick's coronation (1229) as King of Jerusalem, he is said to have placed the crown on his own head.*

KINGDOM OF JERUSALEM REBUILT
BUT RACKED BY BITTER DISPUTES

The success of the Sixth Crusade was part of a short-lived re-establishment of the crusader states of Outremer during the first half of the 13th century. Although the Christians who lived in the restored kingdom were bitterly at odds, for a short while the Kingdom appeared to have a brighter future. But in 1244 control of Jerusalem was lost once more and after this it would not be in European hands again until 1917.

CHRISTIAN DISPUTES

Almost as soon as Frederick had returned to Europe after regaining Jerusalem, in 1229, John of Ibelin overthrew imperial rule in Cyprus and assumed control himself. Frederick for his part was embroiled in fighting papal forces in Italy, and John of Ibelin established himself as the effective king of both Cyprus and Jerusalem.

In 1230 Frederick attempted to deal with this challenge to his authority, sending an army east under the command of Riccardo Filanghieri, Marshal of the Empire, but John defeated the imperial army at the Battle of Agridi in Cyprus on 15 June 1232. In Acre, moreover, the local barons sided with John against Frederick: they formed a commune and elected John their mayor. Nevertheless, Filanghieri established himself in Tyre and in Jerusalem itself.

The conflict continued after Henry of Lusignan came of age as Henry I of Cyprus; in 1234 Pope Gregory IX excommunicated John of Ibelin. John was then killed when his horse fell on him during a campaign against Muslim forces in 1236.

CRUSADE OF 1239–41

A further European crusade, not usually given a number, was called by Theobald I of Navarre (also known as Count Theobald IV of Champagne) and Richard, Earl of Cornwall. In 1239 possession of a large region of Palestine, including

▲ *During the fight for Jerusalem the sanction of the Church was at first seen as a vital component of the struggle.*

Jerusalem, came under dispute once more on the expiry of Frederick II's treaty with Sultan al-Kamil; embarking in that year, Theobald recaptured Ascalon, Beaufort and Safed, but suffered a major defeat by an Egyptian army at Gaza in November 1239 and returned to Europe in 1240 before the arrival from England of Prince Richard, Earl of Cornwall, the younger brother of Henry III of England.

The crusade of 1239–40 was a relatively minor event in the life of Theobald, who is remembered as one of the greatest of aristocratic troubadours and wrote no fewer than 60 surviving lyrics. He was rumoured to have fallen passionately in love with the formidable Blanche of Castile (mother of 'Saint Louis', King Louis IX), and to have poisoned her husband, King Louis VIII; many of his poems are believed to be addressed to Blanche.

When Richard, Earl of Cornwall, arrived in Acre with a fine company of English knights he was welcomed by the Knights Hospitaller and stayed in their accommodation in the city. He then moved on to Jaffa and proposed to its population that they accompany him to Ascalon and help him refortify that place. This they did, and after Richard had rebuilt the defences and arranged for a garrison, he handed over control to the emperor's representative and returned to England. Also during his stay in the Holy Land, Richard negotiated the release of 33 noblemen, 50 knights and many lower-ranking Christian prisoners captured during Theobald's defeat at Gaza; he collected the unburied remains of many killed in the battle and had them buried in the cemetery at Ascalon. He finalized a treaty initially negotiated by Theobald

▼ *At Sidon the crusaders built a sea castle in the 13th century on a small island connected to the mainland by a bridge.*

▲ *This 15th-century illustration shows Christians fighting to retake Jerusalem with bowmen and siege towers to the fore.*

with Sultan as-Salih Ayyub of Egypt that settled wider borders for the Kingdom of Jerusalem than any since 1187.

The Kingdom of Jerusalem appeared to be thriving and have a sustainable future. The ports of Tyre and Acre were very rich, and the Kingdom was also less isolated than previously: Cyprus and the Kingdom of Armenia in Cilicia were Christian neighbours, offering a degree of security – Armenia had even accepted Latin Christianity and religious rule from Rome. But the Latin Christians were too badly split to take advantage of this opportunity: Tyre and Acre, for all their prosperity, existed in a state of open competition that was akin to warfare, while the Templars and Hospitallers even came to blows. In 1244 this future was swept away by the

invasion of Khwarismian Turks, who seized Jerusalem in August that year, and by a cataclysmic defeat of the Kingdom's army by the troops of Egypt at the Battle of La Forbie near Gaza.

THE BATTLE OF LA FORBIE

The sacking of Jerusalem was savage and brutal. Only 300 Christians escaped to tell the story of how the Turks swept into the city, looting and burning the churches. Christians of the crusader states reacted to the loss of Jerusalem in August by making an alliance with al-Mansur of Damascus against Sultan as-Salih Ayyub of Egypt.

An allied Christian–Syrian army drew up at La Forbie commanded by al-Mansur and Walter of Brienne, Count of Jaffa and Ascalon, against a joint force of Khwarismian Turks and Egyptians commanded by a young Turkish soldier named Rukn al-Zahir Baybars (who shortly afterwards would overthrow Sultan

as-Salih Ayyub and found the Mamluk sultanate of Egypt). The battle was launched by Templar charges on 17 October and fought all through that day and the next.

The Christian–Syrian defeat was absolutely crushing: al-Mansur had just 280 survivors out of more than 2,000 cavalry and many more infantry; the Christian knights were virtually wiped out, with only 33 Templars, 27 Hospitallers and three Teutonic knights surviving the slaughter. Among the dead was Armand of Perigord, Grand Master of the Knights Templar. His Hospitaller counterpart, William of Chatelneuf, was captured.

La Forbie was the most severe and significant defeat for the Latin Christians in the Holy Land since the Battle of the Horns of Hattin. Baybars rose to power as the first of the Mamluk sultans of Egypt in 1260 and swiftly drove the Kingdom of Jerusalem almost to extinction, reducing it to a tiny strip of coastal territory.

THE LAST CRUSADES IN THE EAST

For the most part, the news of the fall of Jerusalem to the Khwarismian Turks and the devastating defeat of the armies of Outremer and Damascus at the Battle of La Forbie had little effect in Europe, but it did provoke one very powerful man to plan a military response. In December 1244. Louis IX of France was revered by contemporaries as the embodiment of Christian chivalry, the perfect Christian ruler. He was fiercely devout, a great leader, respected by knights and men-at-arms – but even he could not bring success to the crusading cause. In fact, he led two crusades, the Seventh of 1248–54, and the Eighth of 1270. The Seventh Crusade, to Egypt, ended with a humiliating surrender. The Eighth Crusade, in Tunisia, ended in his death and the abandonment of the enterprise with only a trade treaty with the city of Tunis to show for it. The year after Louis's death saw the expedition traditionally regarded as the Ninth and last Crusade, led by Prince Edward (the future King Edward I of England). This enterprise brought about a ten-year peace treaty between Christians and Muslims in the Holy Land, but it was followed through the 14th and even 15th centuries by further crusading expeditions despatched from Europe to counter the power of the Mamluks.

▲ *Rukn al-Zahir Baybars destroys a Christian-Syrian army at the devastating Battle of La Forbie near Gaza in 1244.*

◄ *After four years' preparation, Louis IX of France embarked on the Seventh Crusade in 1248, heading to Cyprus and then to Egypt.*

CRUSADE IN EGYPT

KING LOUIS IX CALLS THE SEVENTH CRUSADE

King Louis IX declared his intention to lead a crusade to the East in 1245. But he certainly did not rush to war, for he spent no less than four years recruiting and preparing, raising money and even building a special port at the sleepy village of Aigues-Mortes in southern France, before he finally embarked in 1248.

Louis imposed a swingeing tax on the French Church, demanding one-tenth of ecclesiastical revenues for five years, raising 950,000 livres tournois. (The livre tournois, or 'pound of Tours', was one of a number of currencies used in France in Louis's time.) He demanded municipal grants from the towns of his royal domain, raising another 275,000 livres tournois. In all, he raised around 1.5 million livres tournois – a sum so vast that he campaigned in the East for four years before he needed to borrow more money.

FRENCH LORDS

Louis's recruitment campaign resulted in many of France's great lords taking the cross, including: Peter of Vendôme; Hugh X of Lusignan (Count of La Marche); John of Montfort; and Louis's brothers Alphonse of Poitou, Robert of Artois and Charles of Anjou. Many of these great lords' feudal dependants and blood relatives also joined the crusade. Another notable participant who joined the crusade in France was John, lord of Joinville in Champagne, who later wrote a life of King Louis that is a major source for our knowledge of the Seventh Crusade.

The army that finally embarked from southern France in 1248 numbered around 15,000 and included some 2,500 knights as well as 5,000-odd crossbowmen. As many as half of those who travelled received loans or agreed contracts

▲ *The holy warrior-king, as seen by his enemies. This image of Louis IX on horseback is from a 13th-century Egyptian or Syrian brass medallion inlaid with silver.*

from Louis, meaning that they were effectively subsidized by the king. Practical arrangements included the advance purchase of supplies and equipment, and the contracting of 36 ships from Marseilles and Genoa to carry the army.

DEPARTURE

The French crusade army left from Marseilles and from the specially built port and arsenal at the Aigues-Mortes on 25 August 1248 and sailed initially to Cyprus. They landed at Limassol on 17 September, and there united by prior arrangement with various other crusade participants, including Scottish and Italian forces, around 200 English knights led by William, Earl of Salisbury, and barons from Outremer led by Guillaume of Sonnac, Grand Master of the Knights Templar. The crusade leaders agreed that their first target should be Muslim Egypt: the plan was to defeat the sultan's army there before moving against Syria.

◄ *Louis IX of France embarks at Aigues-Mortes on the 7th Crusade. This depiction is from a mid-16th century stained-glass window in Champigny-sur-Veude, France.*

▲ *Encamped before Damietta in June 1249, Louis and his barons pray for the triumphant ending they envisaged for their painstakingly planned enterprise.*

DAMIETTA

Having overwintered on Cyprus, they embarked for Egypt on 14 May 1249. The fleet, which by now numbered as many as a hundred ships, was scattered by a storm, but the royal ships held together and arrived off the beaches near the target of Damietta (modern Damyut) in early June. They saw an Egyptian Muslim army drawn up on land. Disregarding the advice of senior campaigners to wait for reinforcements, Louis led an immediate assault that drove back the Muslim force in the course of a fierce battle on 5 June.

The Muslims retreated along a pontoon bridge of boats to Damietta and that night, in a panic, the Damietta garrison of Bedouin troops and the town's Muslim population fled. The following day, having been alerted to this development by Christians in Damietta, the French army marched in triumph, unopposed across the bridge of boats, into the port.

▶ *This 17th-century Ottoman map shows Muslim power bases around the Mediterranean as well as the movements and origins of crusaders, marking Jerusalem with an image of Christ.*

JOHN, LORD OF JOINVILLE, AND FRIEND OF LOUIS IX

John came from a family of lesser nobles from the Champagne region of France who, nevertheless, had a proud history of crusading – and is a good example of the way taking the cross became a tradition in certain families. John's grandfather, Geoffrey of Joinville, had travelled on the Third Crusade and was killed during the siege of Acre in 1189; John's father, Simon, had crusaded against the Cathars in southern France and fought on the Fifth Crusade, taking part in the capture of Damietta; he also had two uncles who had gone on crusade. John himself took the cross in 1244. In the catastrophic defeat that ended the Seventh Crusade he was later captured with King Louis and travelled with him to Acre, where he became friends with the king before returning in the royal party to France in 1254. He served as seneschal of Champagne, and lived both at the royal court and in Joinville. In 1270 he refused to take part in the ill-fated Eighth Crusade (on which Louis died): before Louis departed, John told him the enterprise was folly. He began writing his life of

▲ *This statue of Louis IX is believed to be true to life. The king was canonized in 1297, just 27 years after his death. He is revered as the perfect Christian king.*

King Louis in the 1270s, but did not complete it until 1309, when it was presented to Louis X. By this time, Louis IX had been canonized and the work was called the *Histoire de Saint-Louis* (The Story of St Louis).

A KING'S RANSOM

THE CRUSADE FAILS AND KING LOUIS IS CAPTURED

After the capture of Damietta on 6 June 1249 the sultan of Egypt, al-Salih Ayyub, offered to swap possession of the town for the Holy City of Jerusalem, as his predecessor al-Kamil had in 1219 and 1221. But Louis rejected the offer, as Pelagius had done before, on the grounds that possession of Jerusalem could not be bartered for. Louis knew, also, that al-Salih Ayyub was seriously ill with tuberculosis and that Egyptian morale was very low. He no doubt believed that with God's help the French army was poised to take complete control of Egypt as a precursor to defeating Muslim Syria and winning Jerusalem.

Initially Louis sat tight in Damietta. It was the start of the season for the flooding of the River Nile, and the king had learned the lessons of the Fifth Crusade when papal legate Pelagius and John of Brienne had been trapped in the Nile mud and forced to surrender. He waited for the waters to subside. In the interim he oversaw the reconsecration of the town's Great Mosque as a cathedral, and the establishment of an archbishopric there. In October, reinforcements from France arrived and the following month, on 20 November, Louis marched towards Cairo.

BATTLE OF AL-MANSOURAH

As the French army proceeded southwards, Sultan al-Salih Ayyub died. In mid-December the crusaders drew up on the bank of the al-Bahr al-Saghir river, opposite the fortress of al-Mansourah, where a 70,000-strong Ayyubid army was encamped. But the crusaders could not find a way across, and remained there for six weeks engaged in the construction

▲ *Louis received Robert of Nantes, the Latin Patriarch of Jerusalem, in Damietta in 1249. The king established an archbishopric in Damietta under the Patriarch's authority.*

of a causeway. Then in early February 1249, a local Coptic Christian alerted them to the existence of an undefended ford a little way downstream, and on 8 February the army's vanguard led the advance on al-Mansourah.

Under the command of Louis's brother, Count Robert of Artois, the French vanguard (with a contingent of Templars and of English knights under Earl William of Salisbury) launched a surprise attack on the Ayyubid camp. The Ayyubid troops fled and Count Robert and his fellow commanders, ignoring orders to wait, and driven by the chivalric urge to glory, rode after them into Damietta. But in the town the Egyptians were rallied by the brilliant commander Rukn al-Zahir Baybars (victor at the Battle of La Forbie) and turned on their pursuers. They cut down the small band of crusaders – who were

◀ *This celebrated portrait of St Louis was painted by Spanish-Greek artist El Greco in c.1592. In Louis's lifetime the French king was the most powerful of the monarchs of Europe.*

▲ *Scenes from a 13th-century book show Pope Innocent IV at the Ecumenical Council of Lyon in 1246 (top left), Louis (top right) receiving the blessing of the church, and the Battle of Gaza, on 12 October 1244.*

disoriented and unable to manoeuvre easily in the narrow streets – in a devastating slaughter. Most of the English knights, including Earl William and all but five Templars, were killed. Count Robert was also slain, with the members of his bodyguard. Through lack of discipline they had thrown away the advantage.

Meanwhile, the main part of the French army was still crossing the ford. Around half the army had crossed when the Egyptians, commanded by Baybars, poured out of Damietta once more to attack. A fierce battle ensued. The crusaders just about managed to hold their ground and finally the Egyptians retreated into al-Mansourah.

SIEGE OF MANY MONTHS

Louis settled in for a siege, hopeful that in the aftermath of the death of Sultan al-Salih Ayyub infighting over the succession would distract the Egyptians from the matter in hand and open the path to a victory for the Christians.

However, a new sultan, Turan Shah, arrived from Damascus to take command, and he quickly imposed his authority on the Egyptian force.

Over the following months the Egyptians effectively undermined the crusader position – principally by venturing out to destroy, one after another, the barges bringing supplies downriver from Damietta. Dysentery and typhoid spread through the crusader camp, and starvation loomed. Louis tried to reopen negotiations, but found that possession of Jerusalem was no longer on offer. His

advisers urged him to make a swift retreat, with just his bodyguard in attendance, but he refused to abandon his army of crusaders to its fate.

RETREAT – AND SURRENDER

On 5 April 1250 Louis accepted the inevitable and ordered a general retreat to Damietta, with the sick going in the front and the remnant of the army marching behind. As they limped northwards, the army was repeatedly attacked by Egyptian horsemen. On only the second day of the march, 6 April, Louis fell seriously ill and became delirious. The army was surrounded, and surrendered.

Under the terms of the surrender, Damietta was returned to the sultan. Those among the crusaders who had been reduced to weakness by disease were killed. Sultan Turan Shah decided there were too many prisoners to control and feed: and ordered that every day for a week 300 of the able-bodied Christians be marched out of the camp and executed. Louis himself was seized and marched in chains to al-Mansourah. The sultan demanded a ransom of 800,000 gold bezants, sending Louis's cloak to Damascus as proof of his triumph.

▼ *The crusade reaches a humiliating end as Louis is captured (left of picture) and then cast into a common jail (right) by his captor.*

THE EIGHTH CRUSADE
KING LOUIS'S FINAL ENDEAVOUR

In the mid-1260s devastating attacks by Egyptian sultan Baybars on Christian holdings in Syria and Palestine reduced Outremer to little more than the port of Acre in Syria. Louis IX of France was inspired by these events to launch another crusade, but it got no further than its very first engagement, the siege of the north African city of Tunis, which had been planned as a preliminary to an attack on Egypt prior to an assault on Muslim strongholds in the Holy Land.

AFTER THE SEVENTH CRUSADE

The failure of the Seventh Crusade in Egypt and the capture of Louis IX by Sultan Turan Shah in April 1250 provoked an outpouring of grief in France. The peasants of northern France rose up in a protest movement that presented itself as a crusade to free their pious king from humiliating captivity among the infidel, but which was really a social uprising and a protest against the failure of the French nobility and the Church to go to Louis's aid (see box).

Meanwhile in May 1251, on the payment of his vast ransom, Louis was released and departed from Egypt, bound for Acre. He stayed in the Holy Land for three years, effectively ruling the Kingdom of Jerusalem and holding his court in Acre. In his time there he refortified Acre, Caesarea, Jaffa and Sidon. He made several diplomatic attempts to improve the standing of the states of Outremer. In April 1254 he had to return to France on the death of his mother, Blanche of Castile, who had been serving as his regent.

OUTREMER UNDER PRESSURE

In the early 13th century Genghis Khan had led a devastating expansion from Mongolia and founded a vast empire. His grandson Hulagu inherited the Mongol territories in Persia and Armenia and in 1260 he captured Damascus.

▲ *Angels lead the way across the waves as the saintly Louis IX embarks on crusade from the port of Aigues-Mortes in France.*

Meanwhile, the general Baybars had risen up against Sultan Turan Shah in Egypt and founded a new sultanate of Mamluks (a military caste of former slaves converted to Islam). Baybars was originally himself a victim of the Mongols: he was a Kipchak Turk from the northern coasts of the Black Sea, who was sold into slavery in Egypt after his lands were overrun by Mongols in c.1240. In the service of the Ayyubid Egyptian sultan al-Salih, he rose to prominence, and defeated crusader armies at La Forbie and al-Mansourah.

In 1260, after taking Damascus, Hulagu sent his principal general, Kitboga, southwards to defeat Egypt. The Mongols met their match in Baybars, who led the Egyptian army to victory in the Battle of Ain Jalut in Galilee on 3 September 1260. That same year Baybars plotted the death of the Mamluk sultan, Qutuz, and seized power for himself. He marched into Syria and took Damascus. He now had control both of Egypt and of Syria and united them in a single state.

In 1265 Baybars repaired and refortified the Syrian fortresses earlier destroyed by the Mongols, then launched an invasion of Outremer. That year he took the town of Caesarea and seized Arsuf from its garrison of Knights Hospitaller. The garrison surrendered on the promise that survivors would be freed, and then were slaughtered to a man. In 1266 Baybars captured Safed from the Knights Templar – again Baybars promised safe passage to members of the garrison, only to behead them. He took Toron, also in 1266. In 1268 he invaded Outremer once more, and captured Jaffa and Antioch. Both were utterly destroyed, their populations either slaughtered or sold into slavery.

LOUIS'S SECOND ATTEMPT

Baybars' devastation of Outremer inspired Louis IX to take the cross a second time, on 24 March 1267. Recruitment this time proved much more difficult than in 1245–48. Nevertheless, three years later Louis embarked from Aigues-Mortes with an army of around 10,000 men bound initially for Sardinia. He was persuaded by his brother, Charles of Anjou, to direct the attack first against Tunis, then to move against Baybars' power base in Egypt.

The crusaders landed in northern Africa in July, and besieged Tunis. Almost at once, a large part of the army became sick after drinking dirty water; Louis himself was struck down so badly that he

▲ *While in Outremer in 1251–54, Louis oversaw the building of fortifications at Caesarea, surrounded by a deep moat.*

died, on 25 August, just one day after Charles of Anjou had arrived to lend his support. By tradition, Louis's dying word was 'Jerusalem!' Louis's 25-year-old son Philip, Count of Orleans, was proclaimed King Philip III of France; Charles of Anjou took on leadership of the crusade.

The crusaders failed to take Tunis. On 30 October they lifted the siege after negotiating a favourable settlement under which Christian merchants could enjoy free trade with the city and priests and monks were given rights of residence there. About this time Prince Edward of England arrived. He moved swiftly on Acre, the only surviving crusader territory in Syria. His actions there are considered to form the Ninth Crusade.

▼ *Louis is struck down by dysentery near Tunis. He died without fulfilling his desire to reclaim the Holy City, and the legend arose that his last word was 'Jerusalem!'*

THE SHEPHERDS' CRUSADE OF 1251

French popular unrest over the capture of Louis IX in Egypt was focused into a protest by a Hungarian monk known as le Maître de Hongrie (The Hungarian Master). He declared that the Blessed Virgin Mary, Mother of Christ, had visited him in a dream with instructions to mobilize the shepherds of France and lead them in a crusade to free the saintly king from captivity.

Chronicle accounts suggest that the 'shepherd' army, which contained all kinds of rural poor, including women and children, numbered 60,000. The monk led them to Paris but Louis's mother, Blanche of Castile, who was acting as regent, sent them on their way.

(English chronicler Matthew Paris met the monk and afterwards declared him an imposter; Matthew believed that the man was a rabble-rouser, and a survivor of the so-called Children's Crusade of 1212.) The crusaders went to Rouen, where they attacked priests, and Tours, where they used violence against monasteries. Later in Amiens and Bourges they attacked Jews. At this point the regent, Blanche of Castile, gave orders that the wandering crusaders be dispersed; in a fight outside Bourges, the Master was killed and his followers then broke up of their own accord. Some of them are believed to have taken the cross and gone to the Holy Land.

THE NINTH CRUSADE

PRINCE EDWARD IN ACRE

Prince Edward of England (the future King Edward I) led an English army to the Holy Land to support the beleaguered remnants of Christian Outremer, principally Acre and Tripoli, in 1271–72. The crusade led to the signing of two ten-year truces with the warlike Egyptian sultan Baybars, and the settlement of disputes between Christians in the Holy Land – but it did nothing to secure the long-term future of Outremer. While in Acre, Edward also famously survived an assassination attempt sponsored by Baybars.

FIRST TO TUNIS

Edward had responded to King Louis IX's calling of a new crusade in response to attacks by Sultan Baybars of Egypt on the few remaining Christian strongholds in the East. He arrived in north Africa too late to take part in that crusade, which came to nothing, and after Louis IX's death of dysentery and the subsequent lifting of the

▼ At Acre the Knights Hospitaller built a formidable citadel, which was part of the north wall of the city. Beneath the citadel they excavated a series of large halls.

▲ Edward was a proven warrior before he went on crusade. At the age of 24, he had commanded the cavalry in the army of his father, Henry III, at the Battle of Lewes.

siege of Tunis in October 1270, Edward and his English knights, together with the remnant of the crusader army commanded by the late king's brother Charles of Anjou, sailed on to overwinter in Sicily before the English contingent alone pressed on to Acre. Edward travelled on crusade with his beloved wife Eleanor of Castile, whom he had married when he was 15 and she was 9 in 1254.

TRIPOLI SAVED

Sultan Baybars's capture of Antioch in May 1268 was as ruthless as any before it: the garrison and population were slaughtered or sold into slavery, the city razed to the ground. It was news of this calamity, which left the crusader County of Tripoli in a very vulnerable position, that inspired Prince Edward to take the cross. When Edward landed in May 1271, Baybars had just taken the formidable fortress of Krak des Chevaliers and was already besieging

Tripoli. But the landing of Edward's army, coupled with crusader expeditions against the Egyptian army's supply lines, caused Baybars to lift the siege and agree a ten-year truce with Tripoli.

EMBASSY TO THE MONGOLS

In June Baybars captured Montfort Castle, near Acre, from the Teutonic Knights; for once he honoured his promise to let the garrison escape alive – he marched them up to the walls of Acre before releasing them. Within the city, the knights and men-at-arms clamoured for Edward to lead a sortie against Baybars and his army – but, seeing the enormous size and strength of the Egyptian sultan's force, Edward elected to stay put. Later in the month Edward led a brief raid on St Georges-de-Lebeyne, a mere 15 miles (24km) from Acre: his army captured and looted the settlement, but the troops were badly affected by food poisoning and extreme heat.

In the same month, June 1271, Edward sent an embassy to the Mongol ruler of Iran, Iraq and parts of Anatolia, Il Khan Abagha, seeking an alliance against Sultan Baybars. While in Acre, Edward also attempted to defuse quarrels among the Christians of Outremer and Cyprus, saying that unless they could present a united front against the military threat of Baybars, they were certainly doomed. For instance, he acted as arbitrator in a dispute between King Hugh III of Jerusalem and Cyprus, and Hugh's knights, members of the powerful Ibelin family, who challenged Hugh's claim that they should fight for him in Outremer as well as in Cyprus.

THE SECOND EXPEDITION FROM ACRE

In the autumn, the Christian position in Outremer was strengthened when Edward's embassy to the Mongols bore fruit in a Mongol attack on Mamluk Syria, and reinforcements from England arrived under the command of Prince Edmund. In November, Edward led a second military expedition from Acre, marching with

▲ *Stabbed by a would-be assassin, Edward overpowered the man and so saved his own life. Acre might have been Edward's place of death, and England would have been deprived of one of its great kings.*

the support of local barons and members of the military orders around 45 miles (70km) to attack the Muslim-held castle of Qaqun. He and his troops won a victory over a Turkoman army but were unable to defeat the garrison and take the castle and retreated again to the safety of Acre. There he oversaw the building of a new tower and the foundation of a new military order, that of St Edward of Acre.

A TRUCE – AND AN ASSASSIN

The following year, in May 1272, King Hugh agreed a truce with Sultan Baybars, establishing that the Kingdom of Jerusalem would maintain its borders for ten years, ten months, ten days and ten hours. According to some accounts, Edward was unhappy at this peace treaty, and did not plan to honour it.

The following month, in any case, Sultan Baybars sent an assassin into Acre

in the guise of a Muslim seeking conversion to Christianity; on 16 June this man managed to get into Prince Edward's quarters and stabbed the prince with a poisoned dagger as he slept; Edward woke, kicked out and won possession of the dagger before killing the assassin.

In the traditional account, Edward's wife Eleanor of Castile then saved his life by sucking the poison from his wound before spitting it out. However, this part of the tale was made up; in truth what happened was that Edward's wound became so badly infected that it threatened his life, and an English doctor performed an operation to cut the diseased flesh away.

Afterwards, Edward prepared to attack Jerusalem, but the news that his father, Henry III, had died, making the prince King Edward I of England, forced him to abandon these plans and head home. On 24 September 1272 Edward and Eleanor embarked for Europe, sailing initially to southern Italy, and travelling home by way of Savoy, Paris and Gascony. They landed in England on 2 August 1274 and Edward was crowned King Edward I of England on 19 August in Westminster Abbey.

THE FALL OF TRIPOLI AND ACRE
THE END OF OUTREMER

The ten-year truces signed by Tripoli and Acre with Muslim Egypt were essentially worthless, for neither Sultan Baybars nor his successors in Cairo were the type of men to be bound by such a nicety as a peace treaty. Following the death of Baybars in 1277, sultans Qalawun and Khalil led the Mamluk Egyptian army to the conquest of Tripoli in 1289 and of Acre in 1291.

CRUSADING INITIATIVES
In the immediate aftermath of the Ninth Crusade there were further attempts in Europe to mount expeditions to come to the aid of Outremer. Pope Gregory X entered negotiations with the Mongols to mount a combined campaign in the Holy Land and preached a crusade in 1274, but the plans came to nothing following

▼ *In Tripoli the forbidding Castle of Raymond of St Gilles, named for the leader of the First Crusade, was expanded by the Mamluks after they captured it in 1289.*

Gregory's death in January 1276. In 1282 Louis IX's brother, Charles of Anjou, King of Sicily and in name King of Jerusalem (after he had bought the succession rights from Mary of Antioch) attempted to mount a campaign to retake Constantinople for Latin Christianity. (Constantinople had been recaptured by the Byzantine Greeks under Emperor Michael VIII Palaeologus in 1261 – *see* box.) But Charles had to abandon the campaign to deal with an uprising against his rule in the War of the Sicilian Vespers.

THE MAMLUK SUCCESSION
In the year of his death, in 1277, Sultan Baybars achieved two final triumphs: the defeat of a combined Mongol–Seljuk Turk army and the capture of Caesarea. When he died in June of that year, Baybars was initially succeeded by his son Baraka, who was forced to abdicate by a revolt in Egypt. He was replaced by Salamish, his seven-year-old brother – then Qalawun, established himself as regent from 1279.

▲ *Acre was held by the crusaders from 1104 until 1187, when it was taken by Saladin, and from 1191 to 1291. For its last century in Christian hands, Acre was the capital of the Kingdom of Jerusalem.*

EVENTS IN OUTREMER
Charles of Anjou died in 1285, and King Henry III of Cyprus was crowned King of Jerusalem at Acre on 15 August 1286. After two weeks of celebrations including an 'Arthurian Round Table' chivalric tournament, Henry returned to Cyprus leaving his uncle, Philip of Ibelin, to rule in Acre as his bailiff. Then, in 1287, Bohemond VIII, Count of Tripoli, died. The citizens of Tripoli chose to become a republic rather than accept the accession of Bohemond's sister Lucia and asked the republic of Genoa to send its fleet.

This was the impetus for Sultan Qalawun to march on Tripoli with a vast army and settle in for a siege. He had earlier moved against the remaining crusader possessions, capturing the Hospitaller fortress of Margat in 1285 and taking the main Syrian port, Latakia, in 1287. The siege of Tripoli lasted less than a month. Qalawun's troops slaughtered the population and destroyed the city and its port so that a new wave of crusaders would have nothing to inherit.

THE RECOVERY OF THE BYZANTINE EMPIRE

Following the sacking of Constantinople in 1204 during the Fourth Crusade, and the establishment there of the Latin empire of Constantinople, the Byzantine Empire moved its capital to Nicaea. There, Constantine Laskaris established a new dynasty of emperors – the Laskarid. This dynasty ruled until 1261, when the child-emperor John IV Laskaris, was deposed by an aristocrat who declared himself Emperor Michael VIII Palaeologus. Emperor Michael captured Constantinople from the final Latin ruler, Baldwin III, on 25 July 1261. Threatened in the 1270s by Charles of Anjou's scheme to reclaim Constantinople under the authority of Rome, Michael offered to engineer the reunification of the Christian Church and to place Orthodox Christianity under papal rule. However, he was unable to force this on his outraged subjects, and had to back down, leading to his excommunication by Pope Martin IV. Michael – and Constantinople – were then saved from attack at the hands of Pope Martin's ally, Charles of Anjou, by the War of the Sicilian Vespers, which Michael himself had secretly incited. Subsequently, Michael continued to reign until his death in 1282: he established the Palaeologian Dynasty of Byzantine emperors, who ruled the empire until the Ottoman Turks captred Constantinople under Mehmed 'the Conqueror' in 1453.

THE FALL OF ACRE

Determined to achieve the destruction of the crusader states, Qalawun next moved against Acre. But he died in November 1290 before he could effect its capture. His son and successor, Khalil, began the siege, bringing an army perhaps 75,000 strong and a huge siege train containing more than 90 mangonels and trebuchets. The siege began on 11 April 1291.

The garrison numbered 800 knights and 14,000 infantry. From Europe came a contingent of English knights sent by Edward I of England under the command of Odo of Savoy, and a contingent of French knights under Jean of Grailly. The defenders manned Acre's double line of walls, with the Templars on the northern section, the Hospitallers alongside them, the French on the southern walls and Venetians, Genoans and Pisans defending the port area. Further reinforcements under King Henry II of Cyprus and Jerusalem arrived on 4 May.

The besiegers set up their great engines: one directed at the quarter defended by the Templars, another aimed at the Hospitallers' area of walls and a third wheeled machine trained on the Accursed Tower, on the eastern wall and defended by knights of Cyprus and Syria.

Early in the siege Frankish envoys rode into the Egyptian camp and spoke to the Sultan, asking him to have mercy on the poor and vulnerable of the city. He made them an offer: abandon the city and he would let them leave freely. They refused to negotiate, perhaps remembering the many promises broken by Sultan Baybars.

The knights of the military orders made two night-time sorties – the first (by the Templars) was essentially successful, although it did not result in the hoped-for destruction of siege equipment, but the second (by the Hospitallers) was met with fierce resistance.

The continual assault by the siege engines and the digging of sappers beneath the walls inevitably had its effect. On 15 May, following the collapse of the towers of Blois, of St Nicholas and of Henry II, the defenders were forced to abandon the outer walls and retreat to the inner defences. On 18 May Sultan Khalil ordered a general assault, which was launched before dawn to the beating of a kettledrum and accompanied by a hail of Greek fire and a storm of arrows. The Accursed Tower was the first to be taken by the attackers, and in the bitter struggle the Grand Master of the Knights Templar, William of Beaujeu, was killed in the fighting. The attackers poured through and overran the city. Acre fell to Sultan Khalil on 18 May 1291. Only a small group of Knights Templar, in the Templars' palace, carried on the resistance – but they were forced to surrender after a week. The population of the city was put to the sword, and its buildings, including the warehouse and port, were utterly destroyed.

END OF OUTREMER

In the days following the fall of Acre, the crusader towns of Beirut, Tyre, Haifa and Tortosa were all abandoned by their defenders. A few thousand refugees managed to escape in ships bound for Cyprus, which remained in crusader hands; other survivors were sold into slavery. A little less than two centuries after the First Crusade, the Latin Christians had been expelled from the Holy Land. Outremer was a thing of the past.

▼ *William of Clermont at the forefront of the last stand in defence of the Kingdom of Jerusalem on the walls of Acre.*

THE ATTACK ON ALEXANDRIA
CRUSADES OF THE 14TH CENTURY

The fall of Acre in 1291 is traditionally taken as the end of the crusades, but people continued to take the cross for centuries afterward. Christian rulers and adventurers made a number of attempts to revive the attack on Islam in the course of the 14th century.

CRUSADING LEAGUES

In the Aegean region, Western powers such as the Knights Hospitaller, Cypriots and Venetian trading colonies attempted to form maritime crusading leagues to combat the power of Turkish emirates that had emerged along the western coast of Anatolia following Mongol devastation of the Seljuk Sultanate. These leagues had papal blessing and assembled small fleets to take the fight to the Turks by sea; they went to war under crusading indulgences and tax exemptions. The first league was formed in 1334 and defeated a Turkish fleet at Adramyttium.

A second league was established ten years later and made a significant capture

▼ *Alexandria's library was established by Ptolemy II in the 3rd century BC. By the time of King Peter's Crusade it was far from the institution it had been. The crusaders claimed that all the books were burned after Muslims conquered the city in AD642.*

by taking the port of Smyrna. In the wake of this, French lord Humbert II, Dauphin of Viennois (the region near Vienne in west-central France), attempted to gather a crusading army in northern Italy to consolidate Smyrna and then take further territory. But his efforts came to nothing, principally because of enduring hostility between the rival trading cities of Venice and Genoa.

A third league was gathered in 1359 and under the papal legate to the East, the French-born Carmelite Peter Thomas, won a victory at Lampsacus, an ancient Greek city on the eastern Hellespont (near Lapseki in Turkey). The league supported the efforts by Peter I of Cyprus to repel the Turkish coastal emirates, which were launching attacks on his territories. Gaining the fortified harbour of Corycus (modern Kizkalesi, Turkey) in 1360, he

▲ *The background to the early 14th-century crusades was the dissolution of the Knights Templar by Pope Clement V (left) in 1312. He transferred the Templars' vast wealth to the Knights Hospitaller, now on Rhodes.*

captured the port of Adalia (now Antalya in south-western Turkey) in 1361, and in 1362 led raids on Myra, Anamour, Siki and other ports along the Mediterranean coast of what is now southern Turkey.

KING PETER'S CRUSADE

Bolstered by these successes, but frustrated that the paucity of Cypriot resources prevented him doing more, he embarked on a tour of Europe in 1362, attempting with papal support to win the backing of European knights and rulers for a crusade. He visited Poland, Bohemia, Germany, France, England and the Low Countries.

The result was the embarkation of a crusading army at Venice on 27 June 1365. The enterprise was called 'King Peter's Crusade' by contemporaries.

The army sailed to Rhodes, where they joined forces with Knights Hospitaller. Peter had heard of plans for an attack from Mamluk Egypt on Cyprus and drew up a plan to pre-empt this campaign by seizing the Egyptian port of Alexandria and then negotiating to swap possession of the Egyptian port for the Holy City of Jerusalem. The combined army, embarked in a fleet of 165 mainly Cypriot and Italian ships, set sail under his command in October 1365 bound for northern Africa.

On 9 October they made a difficult landing under heavy attack from the shore: Muslim bowmen kept up a thick rain of arrows on to the crusader galleys as they neared land and warriors, undeterred by crossbow bolts fired from the ships, came into the sea up to their chests fighting desperately to drive the crusaders off. Finally a brave contingent of Peter's army established a beachhead and began to drive the Muslims back.

The retreating Mamluks closed the city gates and manned the battlements against Peter's invaders. Peter set a great fire before the gates and caused sufficient damage to enable his army to break into the city. An orgy of violence and looting followed. The crusaders rampaged through Alexandria stealing indiscriminately and even sacking the city's celebrated library.

According to the account of French musician-poet William of Machaut, more than 20,000 Saracens were killed in the attack and many others fled. The victory, he claimed, was a triumph for the Christian faith, one ordained by God and given as a reward to King Peter for his dedication to the cause of Christianity.

PETER ABANDONED

But in the aftermath of victory, Peter found that his army of adventurers did not have the stomach to stay and defend what they had won, and virtually to a man they took their booty and departed for home.

William of Machaut reports that the Viscount of Turenne made a speech warning against staying and the crusaders followed his advice. The viscount declared that King Peter did not have sufficient men to defend the city, that his army did not have food, supplies or adequate artillery and that they would soon be faced with an army raised by the sultan of Egypt, al-Ashraf Nasir, who would bring 'five hundred times five hundred thousand men' to win back the city. William notes that Peter was extremely upset, not least because before embarking on the crusade the viscount had promised to serve Peter for a year in defence of any lands conquered on the expedition. Another contemporary comment on the endeavour was made by the great poet Francesco Petrarcha (Petrarch), who wrote to his fellow writer Giovanni Boccaccio that the city of Alexandria, once taken, could have been a great base for Christianity in driving back the Saracens in Africa, but that the enterprise failed because too many of the crusaders were from northern climes – people, according to Petrarch, who begin enterprises full of energy, but cannot carry them through. The crusaders, now immeasurably richer, abandoned Alexandria and headed for home, followed by the exasperated King Peter.

PLANS TO REGAIN THE HOLY LAND

European men of letters of the 14th century drew up a range of plans for re-establishing the Kingdom of Jerusalem. The Venetian Marino Sanuto Torsello, for example, argued that the best means of achieving this end was to outlaw trade with Muslim Egypt: traders would be barred from delivering their cargoes of children, timber and iron to Egypt and from collecting cargoes of sugar, cotton and spices. He pointed out that a similar embargo on sea trade had been imposed in 1187 on trading with the empire of Saladin. He argued that this time the embargo should be maintained on land and sea.

▲ *Sanuto envisaged that after a trade embargo brought Egypt low, Christian knights could win back the Holy Land.*

▼ *This illustration from Sanuto's treatise shows traders carrying supplies to and from the Holy Land.*

PETER I OF CYPRUS

THE CRUSADER KING

Peter of Cyprus is known to history as the crusading king, who briefly in the mid-14th century made Cyprus a major participant in international affairs. He reigned for just 11 years, 1358–69, but established himself as a well-known figure of chivalry, the founder of a chivalric order and leader of holy war against Egypt of 1365. This enterprise was known by contemporaries as 'King Peter's Crusade'.

THE ORDER OF THE SWORD

Peter, sometimes also called Pierre I of Lusignan, was the second son of King Hugh IV of Cyprus and had the title of King of Jerusalem from 1358–69. Born in 1328 in Nicosia, Peter was just 19 when, in 1347, he had a religious vision that inspired him to found the chivalric Order of the Sword. According to the account given by French poet and musician William of Machaut (*see* box), Peter had a vision of a cross floating in mid-air, venerated by many as the cross on which the Good Thief hung. (The Gospels report that Christ was crucified between two thieves, one of whom railed against Christ, but the second of whom rebuked his fellow thief and addressed Christ as Lord; in later Christian tradition he was known as

the 'Good Thief' or St Dismas.) Peter heard a voice addressing him as 'Son' and urging him to wage holy war to regain the lands promised by God to the holy patriarchs; as a result, he founded the Order of the Sword for knights professing a determination to regain the promised land and for men-at-arms with the desire to save their souls. The emblem of the order was a silver sword, set with the point downward to resemble a crucifix, against a blue background and the words 'With this maintain loyalty' inscribed in gold.

Two years later Peter left secretly for Europe with one of his brothers, perhaps with the intention of trying to raise or join a crusade. But his father, King Hugh, tracked the pair down and had them brought back to Cyprus, where he jailed them for having left without permission.

SEA RAIDS

Following his father's abdication in 1358, Peter assumed power and was crowned King of Cyprus and titular King of Jerusalem in Famagusta in 1360. He achieved a number of successes against Muslim Turkish emirs along the eastern seaboard of the Mediterranean. In 1360 he was invited by the citizens of Corycos,

▲ *King Peter's Crusade in 1365 ended is disarray but Peter himself, seen here issuing orders to his men, had a great reputation a military strategist and leader.*

in Armenian Cilicia, to take control of their harbour settlement and protect them against Turkish attacks. Peter accepted and sent a Cypriot force commanded by Robert of Lusignan to defend the port. The city was then besieged by Turkish forces, but the garrison held firm and Corycos was made part of the Kingdom of Cyprus.

Peter was now seen as a threat by the Turkish emirs on the mainland, and these men united to plan a maritime attack on Cyprus. Peter, however, received news of the plan and launched a pre-emptive strike with the help of the Knights Hospitaller on Rhodes, and some European and papal forces. With a fleet of 120 ships, he attacked and besieged Adalia (now Antalya in south-western Turkey) and forced the Turks to sue for peace. He made them pay a yearly tribute to Cyprus.

TOUR OF EUROPE

The following year Peter embarked on a trip to Europe, intending to generate enthusiasm for a general crusade for the

▲ *Pope Urban V told Peter to bring the 1365 crusade to an end after it broke down, and in the wake of violent reprisals against Christian merchants in Egypt and in Syria.*

recapture of the Holy Land. He took part in a succession of chivalric tournaments and was hospitably received by monarchs and princes, but was unable to win the widespread support he had hoped for.

Nevertheless, by 1365 Peter had managed to raise an army of sorts, and he embarked on his crusade against Egypt in October of that year. As we have seen, the enterprise began well, with the taking of the city of Alexandria, but this quickly degenerated into ill-disciplined looting before the crusaders departed for home, refusing to obey Peter's command to march on Cairo. In contemporary accounts of the events, Peter's own participation was highly praised – he was represented not only as an inspirational leader, but also as a brave warrior and a

▶ *Peter was represented (back row, second from right) with Emperor Charles IV and Pope Urban V (third and fourth from right) in Andrea Bonaiuti's fresco of 'The Church Militant' at St Maria Novella in Florence.*

skilled and capable general who achieved what could have been a significant gain for Christendom if he had not been let down by greedy and self-interested troops.

Peter returned to Cyprus, where he continued to mount raids on Turkish holdings along the coasts of what is now Turkey and Syria. He raided Tripoli and was preparing an attack inland, on Damascus, but abandoned that venture after Venetian merchants – afraid of damage to trade – bribed him handsomely not to carry it through. In 1367 he made another trip to Europe, again to try to raise a crusade force, but without success. Increasingly he ruled with an iron hand: when he discovered that his wife Eleanor had conducted an adulterous affair with John of Morphou, Count of Edessa, he embarked on a bitter campaign against her favourite members of the nobility. Some began to question his sanity.

ASSASSINATION AND LEGACY

On 17 January 1369 Peter was assassinated. Two of his knights allowed conspirators – including Philip of Ibelin, lord of Arsuf, and Henry of Jubail – access to the king's bedchamber early in the morning. There, half-dressed, he was repeatedly stabbed, then beheaded and even had his genitals mutilated by an angry knight, James of Nores.

WILLIAM OF MACHAUT

Born in *c*.1300 in Champagne, the poet William of Machaut was in his mid-70s when he wrote his account of the crusade to Alexandria. He was a celebrated figure, who had served one of the great chivalric monarchs of the age, King John of Bohemia. John insisted on fighting on the French side at the Battle of Poitiers in 1356 despite being almost blind and was killed and then honoured by Edward the Black Prince, who took his emblem of an ostrich feather and motto *Ich Dien* (I serve) as his own. William wrote several poems in praise of royal knighthood and also composed many lays and ballads.

Peter's reign was brief and he died a humiliating death. His crusading endeavours achieved little – the only real effect of the attack on Alexandria was to provoke the Sultan of Egypt and damage trade. Nevertheless, because of his devotion to crusading ideals, the fact that he founded a chivalric brotherhood and cut a impressive figure in the courts of Europe (as well as when fighting during the crusade to Alexandria), he was remembered as a paragon of 14th-century chivalry.

CRUSADE TO MAHDIA

ATTACK ON TUNISIA UNITES WARRING CHRISTIANS, 1390

In 1378 the Catholic Church split, in an event known as the Great Schism: there was one pope in Rome and one in Avignon, and the schism continued until 1417 when rule by a single pope was reintroduced. The rival popes combined in 1390, however, to call a crusade against the town of Mahdia, in Tunisia, home to a corsair fleet.

CHRISTIANS DIVIDED

In 1305, at a time when Italy was riven by the papacy's conflict with the Holy Roman Empire, Pope Clement V moved the Roman curia (papal court) from Rome to Poitiers in France, and then in 1309 moved on to Avignon. In 1378 Pope Gregory XI moved back to Rome, but died the same year; there was a dispute over the succession and while Bartolomeo Prignano took power as Pope Urban VI in Rome, in France cardinals elected Robert of Geneva

▲ *John of Gaunt is received by the citizens of Bayonne. John campaigned in Europe in the 1360s–70s, fought with Edward, the Black Prince, in the Battle of Najera (1367) and led a 'crusade' to Portugal in 1386, which ended in a financial settlement.*

▼ *John of Gaunt was the fourth son of King Edward III of England and was father of King Henry IV. Lady Margaret Beaufort, mother of the first Tudor king (Henry VII) was Gaunt's great-granddaughter.*

as a rival pope to rule from Avignon. Robert took the papal name of, Clement VII, and swiftly excommunicated Urban, declaring him to be the Antichrist.

CRUSADES OF THE GREAT SCHISM

In the years following the Great Schism, supporters of the rival popes fought crusades against one another. In general terms, the Avignon pope enjoyed the support of France and her allies Scotland and Castile, while the pope in Rome had the backing of most of the rest of Europe. In 1383 Sir Henry Despenser, Bishop of Norwich in England, a supporter of Rome and a veteran of papal wars in Italy, led a crusade against Louis of Mâle, Count of Flanders and a supporter of Avignon. In a bloody campaign, beginning in May 1383, Sir Henry took Gravelines, Bourbourg, Dunkirk, Diksmuide and other coastal towns, as well as many castles and a fortified church at Veume. He then drove off

an army raised by the Count of Flanders at Dunkirk and laid siege to Ypres. However, the crusade army became bogged down in the siege and after eight weeks, hearing that the French army under Charles VI was approaching, retreated to Dunkirk. In the end, Sir Henry left for England after a negotiated settlement and the crusade came to nothing – although the settlement with Charles VI reportedly made the bishop and his leading knights considerably richer.

A second crusade took place in 1386 when John of Gaunt, 1st Duke of Lancaster, led a campaign in alliance with Portugal on behalf of Rome against Castile. The enterprise doubled as an attempt to enforce Gaunt's claim to the Castilian throne (through his marriage to Constanza, daughter of the late King Pedro I of Castile), and before he left he was formally recognized as King of Castile by King Richard II of England. However, like its forerunner of 1383, this crusade was settled by a financial agreement under which Gaunt abandoned his claim to the Castile in return for a substantial payment.

CRUSADE OF 1390

The warring halves of Christendom were united by proposals for a crusade against Tunisia in 1390. The idea of the crusade came from Genoese traders whose Mediterranean ships had been raided repeatedly by corsairs from the town of Mahdia, Tunisia. The Genoese, supporters of Pope Boniface IX (Urban VI's successor in Rome), won the backing for the project of King Charles VI of France, who supported Clement VII in Avignon. The proposal was then enthusiastically taken up in France and won the backing of both Boniface IX and Clement VII. Contingents joined from the Low Countries, England and Spain to bolster the mainly French and Genoese army. The leader was named as Count Louis of Bourbon.

▼ *Boniface IX, second Roman pope of the Great Schism of 1378–1417, is crowned. The 1390 crusade, which had his backing, showed the benefits of Christian unity.*

The crusaders set sail from Marseilles and went by way of Genoa to northern Africa. They expected to have a fierce fight on their hands when they landed before Mahdia, but they disembarked unopposed and began a siege, with Count Louis's army surrounding three sides of the city by land and the Genoan fleet blockading the seaward wide. The inhabitants of the town waited three days before launching any attack: when it came, it was easily beaten back by Count Louis's troops, who drove the Mahdians back and reached as far as the gates of the city, fighting fiercely, but unable to force their way into the city.

After that the crusade went on for nine weeks, until finally the Genoans negotiated a peace treaty with Ahmad, emir of Tunis, under which the Tunisians would pay handsome taxes to Genoa for 15 years as well as furnishing them with 12,000 gold sovereigns to cover the cost of this campaign. The crusade turned out well for Genoa, but achieved none of its wider goals – although it certainly had benefits for Christian morale at a time of schism. Its success probably lay in the fact that it gave considerable weight to the argument that the disputes of the Great Schism would be best solved not by wars between rival camps but by creating a united front against the Turks. A further crusade would be proclaimed by Avignon and Rome in 1394 – this time against the rising power of the Ottoman Turks.

▲ *In 1417 the Great Schism was over and the Church was reunified with the deposition of two popes, the abdication of a third and the election of Pope Martin V, seen here at the Council of Constance, 1418.*

THE ENDURING SCHISM

The division within Christianity continued, however. Indeed, the two-way split became a three-way one in 1409, when patriarchs, cardinals and bishops at the Council of Pisa declared the Holy See to be vacant and elected Peter Phillarges as Pope Alexander V. Finally in 1417, at the Council of Constance, Pope John XXIII (successor to Alexander V) was deposed, the Avignon Pope Benedict XIII was deposed, Pope Gregory XII abdicated and Pope Martin V was elected as sole pope.

DEFEAT AT NICOPOLIS
THE RISE OF THE OTTOMANS

As the 14th century progressed the Christian powers of Europe were increasingly aware of the rising threat posed by the Muslim Ottoman state as it expanded from its original base in Anatolia into the Balkans and towards the lands of the mighty Holy Roman Empire. In the 1390s the Ottomans, under their great general Bayezid I, took Salonika (modern Thessaloniki) in Greece, blockaded Constantinople and invaded Hungary. The Christian response was a major Venetian–Hungarian crusade, with the backing of both the Avignon and Roman popes, in 1396. It ended in yet another crusading humiliation, a crushing victory for Bayezid and his Ottoman army at the Battle of Nicopolis.

OTTOMAN ORIGINS AND EXPANSION

The Ottomans were descended from Turkmen tribes driven from their homes in Turkestan in the early years of the 13th century by the raids of the Mongols. They took their name from Osman I, who reigned from 1299–1326, and was known

▲ *King Sigismund of Hungary was forced to retreat at Nicopolis and took refuge in Venetian shipping. He was frustrated that the crusaders, refusing to listen to the advice of those familiar with Ottoman battle tactics, brought defeat upon themselves.*

as Uthman or 'Ottoman' in Arabic. He was the son of Ertogrul, chief of a principality in Anatolia based at Sögüt (now in Turkey); Osman greatly expanded the principality, taking a series of towns including Eskisehir, Yenisehir and Bursa from the Byzantine Empire. Osman's son Orhan (r.1324–60) continued the expansion, capturing Nicaea (modern Iznik) in 1331 and Nicomedia (Izmit) in 1334.

In 1341–47 Orhan intervened in a Byzantine succession crisis, providing the military support that enabled John VI Cantacuzenus to overcome his rival John V Palaeologus. As a reward for this, John Cantacuzenus gave Orhan the hand of his daughter, princess Theodora, and allowed him to raid Byzantine lands in Thrace and Macedonia. Under Orhan, and as a result of the policy of John Cantacuzenus, the Ottomans won their first permanent holding in Europe, taking Gallipoli in 1354.

In 1361 Orhan's son, Murad I, captured Adrianople and Philippopolis in Thrace

◄ *The Ottomans became a major naval power, mostly acquiring their ships by theft. They stole an entire fleet from the Byzantines in the course of a daring night raid in 1356 led by Sultan Murad's brother Süleyman.*

and forced the Byzantine emperor (by now John V Palaeologus once more) to become a vassal. Making Adrianople his capital, renaming it Edirne, Murad then expanded deep into Serbia and Bulgaria, making local princes accept him as their overlord.

CRUSADE OF 1366

In 1366 Murad faced a crusade from Venice under the command of Italian nobleman Amadeus of Savoy. This small enterprise, which set sail with just 15 ships and 1,700 troops, was intended to restore Byzantine power in the face of Ottoman expansion and to help John Palaeologus, who was Amadeus's second cousin. Amadeus allied with Francesco I of the Aegean island of Lesbos and together they drove the Turks from Gallipoli; afterwards Amadeus, discovering that John Palaeologus had been taken captive by the Bulgarians, captured the ports of Mesembria and Sozopolis on the

Black Sea and besieged Varna, demanding his release. Finally the emperor was freed and the crusade saw no further action.

THE THUNDERBOLT STRIKES

Murad's son was Bayezid I, nicknamed *Yildirim* (the Thunderbolt) for the speed of his military campaigns. He came to power following the death of Murad in battle against Bosnian, Serbian and Bulgarian princes at Kosovo in 1389, and just two years later began a siege of Constantinople, the principal buffer between the Ottoman power base in Anatolia and Europe. He also began to extend Ottoman power towards and into Europe, capturing most of the Balkans and expelling Bulgarian tsar Ivan Shishman from his capital, Nicopolis.

A crusade was proclaimed by both Pope Boniface IX in Rome and his rival, the Avignon pope Clement VII. Kings Richard II of England, Charles VI of France and Sigismund of Hungary (who was later to be Holy Roman Emperor, 1433–37) backed the enterprise: initially the plan was for Charles and Richard to fight on the crusade, but in the event an army of 10,000 French, 1,000 English and around 6,000 from the German states gathered under Sigismund in Buda (now part of the Hungarian capital Budapest) in

▼ *The Battle of Nicopolis became a rout. Admiral of France, Jean of Vienne, fought off attackers trying to capture the French standard six times. In the end he was killed.*

TAMERLAINE AND BAYEZID

The seemingly invincible Bayezid met his match in the Turkish–Mongolian warlord Timur, or Tamerlaine. In 1402 Bayezid again abandoned his siege of Constantinople to deal with a trouble-some enemy, but this time was heavily defeated by Tamerlaine at the Battle of Ankara. Bayezid was taken prisoner and kept in captivity by Tamerlaine.

Colourful contemporary reports suggested that the Ottoman sultan was kept chained in a cage but this is thought to be false. Bayezid certainly died in captivity, however, one year later; his sons, who had escaped to Serbia after the Battle of Ankara, were later able to re-establish Ottoman rule. In the 16th century English playwright Christopher

▲ *Bayezid died after a year in captivity.*

Marlowe wrote a celebrated play, *Tamburlaine the Great*, about the war-lord's exploits. He was also the hero of an opera of 1724, *Tamerlano*, by Handel.

July 1396. The plan was to force the Turks from the Balkans, relieve the siege of Constantinople, and then march across Anatolia and Syria to take Jerusalem for Christ. Mircea, Prince of Wallachia, joined the crusade with a substantial army despite being an Orthodox Christian rather than a Roman Catholic; a contingent from Transylvania also joined up. Venetian and Genoese fleets and a contingent of Hospitaller knights from Rhodes also arrived to lend their support.

The army marched southwards, pillaging towns and massacring locals, before settling in to a siege of Nicopolis, the

Bulgarian capital recently taken by the Turks. Bayezid then showed why he was called 'the Thunderbolt', acting with astonishing decisiveness and speed in lifting his siege of Constantinople and marching against the crusade army. He met them in battle near Nicopolis on 25 September.

Wallachian prince Mircea, who was familiar with Ottoman tactics and had won previous victories against Bayezid, proposed that he should lead an initial assault with his skilled Wallachian light cavalry prior to a main charge by the Western army. But the crusade leaders were suspicious of his motives and instead chose to make a full-scale frontal assault. The battle was a disaster for the crusaders: although the French knights won initial successes against the Ottoman vanguard, they were overwhelmed by the main bulk of Bayezid's men; the Wallachians and Transylvanians deserted and Sigismund escaped. It was a triumph for Bayezid serving to consolidate the Ottomans in the Balkans, and leaving Constantinople even more vulnerable. Bayezid built the magnificent Ulu Mosque in Bursa to commemorate his victory in what became known as the Crusade of Nicopolis.

THE END OF BYZANTIUM

CRUSADERS FAIL TO SAVE CONSTANTINOPLE

The Ottomans repeatedly threatened Constantinople, and Western powers sent intermittent expeditions to the aid of the city. The most significant, in 1444, ended in another heavy defeat for the crusaders at Varna. Then, on 29 May 1453, the Ottomans under Sultan Mehmed II 'the Conqueror' captured Constantinople, marking the end of the Byzantine Empire.

CRUSADES OF BOUCICAUT

French knight Jean Le Meingre, Marshal of France and known as 'Boucicaut', had taken part in the Christians' defeat by Ottoman sultan Bayezid at the Battle of Nicopolis in 1396. Boucicaut was captured in the battle and later ransomed. Then, in 1399, the same year in which he established his chivalric order, the *Emprise de l'Escu Vert à la Dame Blanche* (Enterprise of the Green Shield of the White Lady), he sailed once more to the East. With 21 galleys, three transports and six ships and around 1,200 men, he succeeded in lifting the Ottoman blockade of Constantinople and rescuing the embattled Byzantine emperor, Manuel II

Palaeologus. Manuel then returned with Boucicaut to Europe to try to drum up interest for a further crusade.

In 1401 Boucicaut was made French Governor of Genoa and in 1403 he sailed to Rhodes with a fleet of 16 Genoese ships and from there led a series of raids against ports in Anatolia and Syria held by the Ottomans and the Mamluk Sultanate of Egypt. He attacked Ottoman Alanya in Anatolia, then (with the help of the Knights Hospitaller from Rhodes) raided Mamluk-held Batroun, Tripoli and Beirut.

A NEW CRUSADE

In 1443 Pope Eugenius IV (ruled 1431–47) issued a rallying call to Christians in the West to go to the aid of their brethren in the East against the Ottomans. Murad II, grandson of Bayezid 'the Thunderbolt', had re-established Ottoman supremacy after a period of decline and in-fighting following Bayezid's defeat by the Turkish-Mongolian general Tamerlaine in 1402 and his subsequent death in captivity. Murad II defeated two rivals, forced the Byzantine Empire to pay

▲ *Pope Eugenius IV did much to restore the power of the papacy after the Great Schism. The crusade he called in 1443 almost ended in success at Varna in 1444.*

tribute, and in 1430 recaptured Salonika (Thessaloniki) from the Venetians. Then he annexed Serbia in 1439.

However, the Hungarian army, commanded by King Ladislas of Hungary and his illegitimate son Janos Hunyadi, known as the 'White Knight', won victories against the Ottomans at Nis, Sofia and Snaim in 1443, on the celebrated 'long campaign', and again at Jalowaz in 1444, encouraging Christendom to dream once more of a lasting victory over Islam. A motley collection of crusaders gathered in the Balkans in 1444: the force included Hungarians, Poles, Germans, Ukrainians, Lithuanians, Croatians, Bulgarians and Bosnians. The plan was for a fleet of Genoese, Venetian and papal ships to blockade the Dardanelles to prevent Murad crossing from Anatolia into Europe to fight the crusaders; the fleet and the crusader army would rendezvous at Varna in Bulgaria, then march and sail down the coast of the Black Sea to Constantinople and relieve the siege there, pushing the Ottomans out of Europe in the process. However, the blockade of the Dardanelles failed, and Murad marched to meet the crusaders at Varna.

BATTLE OF VARNA

In the Battle of Varna on 10 November 1444 Murad's Ottoman army of around 60,000 men faced a much smaller crusade army of no more than 20,000 troops commanded by Ladislas and Janos Hunyadi. Not only were the Christians outnumbered, but they also had an unbalanced army, with very few foot soldiers and a great preponderance of heavy cavalry.

The Christians pinned their hopes on the arrival of reinforcements by sea from Constantinople. The papal legate on the crusade, Cardinal Julian Cesarini, called on the army to retreat, but they were in a difficult position, trapped by the enemy between the Black Sea, Lake Varna and the hills. The cardinal then proposed that they attempt to defend their position until they were relieved by Christian reinforcements, but Ladislas and Janos Hunyadi argued for attack – famously declaring: 'Escape is not possible, surrender inconceivable, so let us fight bravely and do honour to the arms we bear!'

The plan almost worked. The crusaders came close to victory: a group of around 500 Polish knights smashed the centre of the Ottoman deployment, breaking through the elite Janissary infantry; Sultan Murad began to flee on horseback but a soldier seized his reins to prevent him, and Murad regained his composure; Janos Hunyadi and his cavalry devastated a company of Sipahis (Ottoman cavalry) and drove them from the battlefield; King Ladislas went in pursuit of Murad, but was cut down by the Ottoman imperial

▶ 'The White Knight' Janos Hunyadi was a formidable opponent of the Ottomans for 20 years from the 1430s to his death in 1456. He was regent of Hungary in 1446–53.

bodyguard, also of Janissaries. Ladislas was beheaded on the battlefield and, seeing the king cut down, the Polish cavalry lost heart and retreated. Janos Hunyadi escaped. King Ladislas's head was subsequently carried off to the Ottoman court.

SECOND BATTLE OF KOSOVO

In 1448 Janos Hunyadi raised another mainly Hungarian Christian army and fought Murad II again, in the Second Battle of Kosovo, which ran over two days in October. (The clash is known as the Second Battle of Kosovo to distinguish it from the earlier battle at the site between a Serbian army led by Prince Lazar and an Ottoman force under Murad I in 1389 – the battle in which Murad I died.)

Once again, as at Varna, Hunyadi was badly outnumbered by Murad II's Ottoman army, and once again he almost won the battle despite this numerical disadvantage; and, as at Varna, it was the

resilience and bravery of the sultan's elite Janissary corps that won the day. The battle began with an attack by Hunyadi's flanks that was driven back, but this was followed by a strong assault by the main part of his army. This defeated the Janissaries and reached as far as the Ottoman camp before falling back; during this latter part of the battle, with Hunyadi's forces retreating, the Janissaries recovered from their earlier setback and delivered a powerful attack that killed many of the finest Hungarian knights and forced Hunyadi himself to flee. Fighting went on with missiles and artillery fire through the night; on the next day the Ottomans launched a final and decisive attack.

The Christians' defeat in this battle left the Ottomans in the ascendant in the Balkans, with the Byzantine Empire at their mercy. Within five years, Murad II's son and successor, Mehmed II 'the Conqueror', had captured Constantinople.

THE CONQUEROR

OTTOMAN SULTAN MEHMED II

Mehmed II, son of Murad II, was celebrated as 'the Conqueror' because he achieved the long-standing Ottoman ambition of taking Constantinople. He was just 21 when he led Ottoman troops into the city on 29 May 1453. On that day the city of Constantine, founded as New Rome in AD330 to be a new capital for the Roman Empire, and for centuries the centre of the Christian Byzantine Empire, became the Islamic city of Istanbul, capital of the Ottoman Empire. The venerable 6th-century Hagia Sophia (Church of Holy Wisdom) was made into a mosque. The leaders of the West were appalled.

BOY EMPEROR

Mehmed II first came to the throne at the age of 12 in 1444. His father Murad II, having suffered defeats at the hands of the Hungarian-led Christian alliance in the Balkans, notably at Jalowaz in 1444,

▼ *Constantinople, former capital of the eastern Roman Empire, falls to Mehmed's troops. By tradition the conquest was foretold by the Prophet Muhammad.*

signed a ten-year peace treaty at Edirne in June 1444. The Western powers then broke the treaty and gathered a crusading army. Murad – who had retired to rural contemplation – returned to power and led the Ottomans to decisive victories over the Christians at Varna in 1444 and in the Second Battle of Kosovo in 1448.

EYES SET ON CONSTANTINOPLE

In 1451 Murad died, and Mehmed became sultan for a second time. Almost at once, in spring 1452, he set about preparing to capture Constantinople. He had a vast cannon cast, raised an army of no fewer than 250,000 Janissaries and built a fleet of 280 ships.

Constantine had barely men enough to defend the walls of the city when Mehmed began his siege on 6 April 1453, and the siege seemed destined to succeed. According to Niccolo Barbaro, a ship's doctor from Venice who was an eyewitness to these events, those in the city became convinced that the Ottomans would succeed after a portent was seen on the night of 22 May 1453: it was a time of

▲ *Rumeli Hisari, the great fortress Mehmed built in 1452 on the European side of the Bosphorus, was also known as 'strait blocker' because it dominated the sea.*

full moon, but the moon rose as a crescent before becoming full later in the night. Outside the walls the besiegers rejoiced, for the Ottomans held the crescent moon to be their symbol.

Mehmed delivered a stirring speech in which he reminded his troops of the greatness of their forebear Bayezid the Thunderbolt. He spoke of their suffering after Bayezid's defeat by Tamerlaine, and of how the Byzantine Empire had played, and continued to play, a major part in all their woes, constantly seeking to create dissension and set Turks against one another. And all the warriors acclaimed him and cheered his plan to attack.

THE CITY TAKEN

At Mehmed's command the Ottoman army began its assault at sunset on 28 May, with the setting sun at their backs shining directly into the faces of the defenders. The assault began with a

terrifying cacophony of pipes, cymbals and trumpets, followed by a barrage of arrows and missiles. Then the walls were attacked and close hand-to-hand fighting followed around the city perimeter. Fighting continued through the night. A Genoese soldier named Giustinianni was leading the defence of the city and when he was shot and fell down dead the defenders around him fled.

At dawn on Tuesday, 29 May 1453, Mehmed himself led a fresh wave of attacks, clasping an iron club, with the Janissaries behind him and at their back a corps of executioners ready to put to death by beheading anyone who attempted to flee. Constantine XI, last in the long line of Byzantine emperors, was killed attempting to prevent this last part of the assault.

The city secured, Mehmed later made a formal entry on horseback at around noon. He entered the Hagia Sophia; it is said by tradition that when he made his way into the Palace of the Caesars, established more than a millennium earlier by Constantine the Great, he quoted from Persian poetry: 'The spider makes his frail curtains in the grand palace of the Caesars, the owl calls softly the watches of the night in the towers of Afrasiab.'

CONQUESTS AND REFORMS

The capture of Constantinople was only the first of Mehmed's many military victories. He went on to conquer Serbia, Bosnia, Albania and Greece, and the great part of the territory around the Black Sea.

▲ *Byzantium, forerunner of Constantinople, was founded by Greek traders. Mehmed visited Troy and announced that he had avenged the Trojans when he beat the Byzantine descendants of the Greeks.*

In 1480, poised to invade Italy, he sent a vast Turkish fleet to besiege the island of Rhodes, stronghold of the Knights Hospitaller. Here he met his match, and after a three-month siege was forced to abandon the attempt to capture the island, having lost no fewer than 9,000 men in the assault. That same year he died.

As well as being a great general, Mehmed was a notable administrator. He rebuilt the city of Constantinople and brought in a new tax system, promulgated a new law code, and set up a group of advisers known as the *ulama* (meaning 'wise' in Arabic), all of whom were fluent in Arabic and Persian as well as Turkish and were learned in Islamic holy law.

Mehmed died in 1481 and was succeeded by his son Bayezid II, who led the Ottomans to a series of further triumphs against Poland, Hungary, Venice, Egypt and Persia (Iran).

◄ *After taking Constantinople, Mehmed II claimed the title of 'Caesar' for himself, implying that the Ottomans were by virtue of conquest rightful heirs of ancient Rome.*

DRACULA

In 1462 Mehmed had an encounter with Prince Vlad III the Impaler. That year Mehmed invaded Wallachia in an attempt to remove Vlad, who had raided Ottoman territory and killed 20,000 people; Mehmed brought a great army with him, and occupied the Wallachian capital, but Vlad kept up a fierce guerrilla war against the invaders. In one incident on the night of 16–17 June Vlad entered the Ottoman camp with his men and came close to assassinating Mehmed. Subsequently, Mehmed installed Vlad's brother Radu, in power. Vlad (below) was the historical basis for Dracula, the fictional vampire created by Bram Stoker in his 1897 novel.

THE MIRACLE OF BELGRADE

CRUSADERS SAVE HUNGARY, 1456

After capturing Constantinople on 1453, the Ottomans under their war-like sultan Mehmed II continued to seek new conquests, both for the glory of Islam and the enrichment of their empire. But the Christian West was encouraged once more to believe in the power of holy war when a makeshift crusading army raised by the sermons of a Franciscan friar named Giovanni da Capistrano succeeded in turning back the Ottomans at the siege of Belgrade in 1456. This event was celebrated as the 'miracle of Belgrade'.

BELGRADE FORTIFIED

The 'White Knight' Janos Hunyadi, great foe of the Ottomans in the early 1440s, was an illegitimate son of the late King Ladislas and had been regent of the Kingdom of Hungary since 1446. He foresaw that Mehmed would move to conquer Hungary, and that to do so the Ottoman

▼ *Mehmed II brought a vast army, heavy artillery and a sizeable fleet to take Belgrade. The unlikely Christian victory seemed a triumph of faith that began to restore belief in the crusading enterprise.*

army would have to take the border fortress of Belgrade (today the capital of the Republic of Serbia). He set about strengthening its defences and laying in provisions, and raised a sizeable garrison force that he placed under the command of his brother Mihaly Szilagyi and his own son Laszlo. He also raised a relief force and a fleet of 200 light warships. His army consisted mainly of battle-hardened mercenaries and a selection of mounted knights from the European nobility.

He was helped in these preparations by the Italian-born Franciscan friar Giovanni da Capistrano. This venerable figure had been used widely by earlier popes as a legate and had preached vehemently against heresies, notably those of the followers of Jan Hus in Bohemia; in 1454, at the age of 70, he was sent by Pope Nicholas V to preach a crusade against the Ottomans at the Diet of Frankfurt. The following year Giovanni was sent by the pope to Hungary and Transylvania to preach the crusade.

There he managed to raise an army and it marched, with Capistrano himself at the head of one division, to support Janos Hunyadi. Capistrano's army consisted of a motley crew, many of them yeomen, armed with scythes and slings, but they were driven and inspired by the preacher's words to believe that God would deliver victory in return or their faith.

SIEGE SET

Mehmed II brought an army of around 70,000 and began his siege of Belgrade on 4 July 1456. He also had 300 cannon and he used his 200 ships to prevent the arrival of reinforcements and supplies by way of the river Danube. The garrison was well armed and motivated but numbered only around 7,000.

The relief army under Janos Hunyadi and Giovanni da Capistrano arrived at Belgrade on 14 July. That same day they

▲ *Franciscan friar and crusade preacher Giovanni da Capistrano raised an army of ill-armed peasants to defend Belgrade. One in a long line of militant churchmen, he led the troops himself into the battle.*

managed to break through Mehmed's naval blockade of the city, sinking a total of seven large and 20 smaller Ottoman ships. They were able to bring troops and supplies into the city. Mehmed then launched a week-long bombardment by his artillery and on the evening of 21 July ordered an all-out attack.

NIGHT FIGHT

The Ottoman attack continued through the night, with desperate fighting on both sides. The Christians managed to hold the attackers at bay and a large contingent of Mehmed's elite Janissaries were put to the sword. In one celebrated incident, a Turkish soldier tried to raise the sultan's banner on a bastion of the fortress when a Hungarian soldier named Titus Dugovic attacked him and the two men fell together from the wall – Dugovic was later celebrated as a hero and his son was raised to the nobility.

On the following day the large body of peasant crusaders that Giovanni da Capistrano had raised took matters into their own hands, launching an impromptu attack on the besieging army. Giovanni da Capistrano tried to call them back, but finding it impossible to impose discipline rode into the conflict himself, reputedly declaring 'The Lord God, who brought about this beginning, will see to the end!' Janos Hunyadi also led a lightning attack, aiming to seize Turkish artillery positions. The main part of the Ottoman army fled.

OTTOMANS SHAMED

The sultan's bodyguard fought heroically, but were overwhelmed by Hunyadi's cavalry. Mehmed delivered a fatal blow to a Christian knight, but then was shot in the leg by a bowman and fell unconscious on the battlefield. Shortly afterwards darkness fell, and by night the Turks lifted the siege and retreated. They needed 140 wagons

▼ *Christians triumph at Belgrade. Pope Calixtus III ordered the church bells to be rung as a call to arms, but it became a celebration. The battle is commemorated to this day by the ringing of a noon bell.*

to bear their wounded away from the city they had expected to take with ease. One of them was Mehmed, still unconscious.

The sultan recovered in the city of Sarona. Contemporary reports tell that he was plunged into despair when he learned that the Ottoman army had been so completely humiliated and so many of his greatest warriors had lost their lives, and had to be prevented by his aides from taking his own life with poison. He then retreated to Constantinople.

▲ *In the 1480s Western powers tried to destabilize the Ottomans by supporting Cem, brother of Bayezid II, seen here meeting with the Knights Hospitaller.*

AFTERMATH OF BELGRADE

The Christian West rejoiced. The relief of the city against all odds evoked the spirit of the First Crusade, when unexpected victories convinced knights and churchmen that their battle was blessed by God. Janos Hunyadi and Giovanni da Capistrano believed that the time was a ripe for a crusading push to drive the Ottomans back, to take Constantinople and perhaps even go on to regain Jerusalem. However, neither man lived to further these ambitious plans. Both fell victim to bubonic plague: Janos Hunyadi died on 11 August, three weeks after the victory; Giovanni da Capistrano followed on 23 October.

Pope Pius II (ruled 1458–64) was inspired by the victory to call a new crusade on 26 September 1459 in Mantua. The following January he proclaimed the crusade for a period of three years. But despite the 'miracle of Belgrade' there was little enthusiasm among the powers of Western Europe and the expedition came to nothing after Pius died in August 1464.

THE WARRIOR MONKS

On 1 May 1187 a small Christian force of foot soldiers and 140 knights under Gerard of Ridefort, Master of the Knights Templar, encountered a Muslim Ayyubid army of 7,000 in the Battle of Cresson near Nazareth. When the Ayyubid horsemen feigned a retreat Gerard rashly ordered a charge, his knights were isolated from the foot soldiers and the two parts of the army cut down. The account in the crusade chronicle *Itinerarium Regis Ricardi* (The Voyage of King Richard) describes the extraordinary heroism and death of Templar knight Jakelin of Mailly, who reportedly fought to the last, surrounded by Muslim soldiers and entirely alone, until he sank to the ground and his soul rose at once to heaven, wearing a martyr's crown and covered in glory.

The Knights Templar and other monastic military brotherhoods – such as the Knights Hospitaller, the Teutonic Knights, the Knights of St Lazarus or the Knights of St Thomas Acon – were famed for their ferocity in battle and the powerful commitment to the crusading cause celebrated in the account of Jakelin of Mailly's death. In battle, they provided a highly disciplined, well-trained fighting force, although their leaders often were drawn by overconfidence or the desire for glory into rash and even disastrous acts. The monastic military brotherhood – consisting of men who like Jakelin of Mailly sought salvation through their exploits in religious warfare – was an institution unique to European chivalry of the Middle Ages, without counterpart in other cultures or eras.

▲ *At Cresson in 1187, Templar Jakelin of Mailly fought to the end.*

◄ *The defence of Rhodes by Fulkes of Villaret and the Knights Hospitaller, against Sultan Osman I in 1307. The Knights held the island until 1522.*

KNIGHTS OF ST JOHN
FOUNDATION AND EARLY YEARS OF 'THE HOSPITALLERS'

The monastic order of the Knights Hospitaller of St John of Jerusalem was established in the wake of the First Crusade with responsibility for the defence of the Holy Land. It had its origins in a hospital or hospice (guesthouse) founded in Jerusalem to care for Christian pilgrims, and was formally recognized in a papal bull of 15 February 1113 issued by Pope Paschal II (ruled 1099–1118).

Paschal's bull gave the order the name of the 'Hospitallers of St John of Jerusalem', but its members were often referred to as 'Knights of St John' or 'Knights Hospitaller', and over the centuries the order has also had many other names – including the 'Knights of Rhodes' and the 'Knights of Malta', reflecting the Hospitallers' residence on those islands. (The order's modern name, in use since the introduction of a new constitution in 1961, combines all these in the title of the 'Sovereign Military Hospitaller Order of St John of Jerusalem'.)

▼ The order of the Knights of St John was founded after the First Crusade and the triumphant gain of Jerusalem.

ORIGINS OF THE HOSPITAL

The hospital in Jerusalem was established by merchants from Amalfi and Salerno in Italy in 1023, with permission from Caliph Ali az-Zahir of Egypt, who ruled Jerusalem at the time. Benedictine monks served the establishment, housing and caring for the pilgrims who came to see the holy sites in Jerusalem. The hospital

▲ The brothers built the imposing Church of St John of the Hospitallers in Sidon in the 13th century. Today it is a mosque.

became associated with St John because it stood close to the site of the monastery of St John the Baptist.

The Jerusalem hospital, in fact, had a long history prior to the 11th century. Its forerunner was established as early as AD600 by a certain Abbot Probus, on the authority of Pope Gregory the Great (ruled 590–604), and was intended from the start to house and care for Christian pilgrims to the Holy Land. Then, in *c.*800, Charlemagne, the King of the Franks, promoter of learning and 'August Emperor', who wanted to establish himself as ruler of all Christendom, expanded the hospital and installed a library there. But in 1010 the hospital was destroyed as part of the demolition of many Christian shrines – including the Church of the Holy Sepulchre – ordered by the sixth Fatimid caliph of Egypt, Al-Hakim bi-Amr Allah. The building raised by the Italian merchants in 1023 was the replacement for the earlier hospital.

▲ *Raymond du Puy was the order's second Grand Master but the first to use the title. He was the man who established the Hospitallers on a firm footing. He fought in the siege of Ascalon in 1153.*

FOUNDER OF THE ORDER

In the immediate aftermath of the capture of Jerusalem by the soldiers of the First Crusade in 1099, a Christian knight or merchant named Gerard Thom became guardian, or superior, of the hospital. Later known as 'Blessed Gerard', he founded the religious order of St John of Jerusalem, under the Benedictine rule, and then travelled to Europe to raise money and gather support – crucially winning the backing of Pope Paschal II. Paschal decreed that the order would not be subject to the authority of the King of Jerusalem, but was to be subservient only to the papacy; he granted it exemption from paying tithes to the Church and the right to own its religious buildings.

Gerard also established associated hostels for pilgrims at cities in Provence and Italy that were on the pilgrim route to the Holy Land. In the Holy Land, the warrior

▶ *The Knights Hospitaller wore the eight-pointed Maltese cross. This example is on a coin issued by John of Brienne, King of Jerusalem in the years 1210–1225.*

monks of the order branched out from housing and caring for pilgrims into providing them with an armed escort on dangerous parts of their journey, when they were liable to attack by bandits or enemy soldiers.

SECOND GRAND MASTER

Gerard was succeeded as Grand Master of the order in 1120 by French knight Raymond du Puy of Provence. Raymond was related to Adhemar of Le Puy, papal legate on the First Crusade, and was the son of the leading crusade knight Hughes du Puy, who fought as a general of Godfrey of Bouillon and was named Governor of Acre. Over 40 years as Grand Master (1120–60), Gerard established the order as a significant military force: he divided the brothers into military, medical and clerical divisions; he established the

order's first infirmary in Jerusalem, close to the Church of the Holy Sepulchre; and he moved the order from the Benedictine to the Augustinian rule.

Gerard also made the eight-pointed cross of Amalfi in Salerno the order's symbol, in honour of the hospital's founders from that town. This symbol later became known as the Maltese cross because of the residence of the Hospitallers on the island of Malta after 1530. The knights went into battle wearing black surcoats marked in white with the eight-pointed cross.

EQUESTRIAN ORDER OF THE HOLY SEPULCHRE OF JERUSALEM

The Equestrian Order of the Holy Sepulchre of Jerusalem is a chivalric order that, like the Order of the Knights of St John, traces its history back to the time of the First Crusade. At that time, Godfrey of Bouillon, the first ruler of the Kingdom of Jerusalem, gathered a body of knights to protect the canons in the Church of the Holy Sepulchre. They fought under the banner of a red cross on a white background. In 1113 Pope Paschal II gave the order official recognition, and in 1122 Pope Callixtus II granted it status as a lay religious order with the duty to defend the Church of the Holy Sepulchre and the city of Jerusalem against attack by Muslims.

▶ *Godfrey, lord of Bouillon, first leader of the Kingdom of Jerusalem, is recognized as the founder of the Equestrian Order.*

HOSPITALLERS SAVE RHODES

KNIGHTS OF ST JOHN DEFEAT MEHMET THE CONQUEROR

After the loss of Jerusalem in 1187 the Knights of St John removed to Acre and, following the fall of Acre in 1291, took up residence on the island of Cyprus, so maintaining a presence in the East. The Hospitallers did not stay long in Cyprus. Within 20 years they had transferred to the island of Rhodes, where they would remain for more than 200 years, in that time twice defeating seaborne armies – one in 1444 from Muslim Egypt and a second in 1480 from the Ottoman sultan Mehmet II 'the Conqueror'.

ESTABLISHMENT ON RHODES

On being driven from the Holy Land following the fall of Acre in 1291, the leading figures in the hierarchy of the Hospitallers saw that the sea would inevitably play an important part in the order's future. The admiral of the Hospitaller fleet, Fulkes of Villaret, joined the inner council of the order in 1299. In 1307 the knights captured Rhodes, in part to curb the operations of Muslim corsairs who used the island as a base of operations for raiding Christian shipping in the East, but also perhaps with an eye to establishing their own landholding.

The knights found it difficult to maintain their independence from court politics on Cyprus and elected to move permanently to Rhodes in 1310. By now Fulkes of Villaret was Grand Master. The order also took control of a number of small neighbouring islands, including Bodrum and Kastellorizo. Using these bases, the Hospitaller knights waged a determined sea war against Muslim corsairs from northern Africa who preyed on Christian shipping in the western Mediterranean. (These ruthless Muslim operators were also known as 'Barbary pirates' because the north African coast from which they emanated was called the Barbary coast.)

The Hospitallers also took part in the various minor crusades of the 14th cen-

▲ *The Ottoman fleet, commanded by Palaeologos Pasha, approaches Rhodes, at the top right of this picture. The island appears secure behind stout walls.*

tury, notably those of 1345 in which Smyrna was captured; 'King Peter's Crusade' of 1365, which degenerated into the sacking of Alexandria; and the Nicopolis Crusade of 1396.

A NEW ORGANIZATION

In this period, the order also became immeasurably richer: after the Knights Templar were disbanded in 1312, all their property was assigned to the Hospitallers by Pope Clement V (ruled 1305–14). The Hospitallers organized their new territory well, dividing their landholdings into eight *langues*, or 'tongues' (Provence, Italy, Germany, France, England, Castile, Auvergne and Aragon), each with its own prior and with key positions of authority in the order distributed among the langues. In this way, the Knights Hospitaller avoided difficulties caused by national feelings at a time when such feelings were increasingly powerful in Europe.

On Rhodes the brothers of different langues lived in their own *auberges*, or hostels, within an enclosed area of the city known as the *collachium*. They fortified both the city and the island's main harbour and established a commercial area, as well as inviting Latin and Greek farmers from the mainland to settle.

ATTACK ON RHODES

In 1426 Cyprus was conquered by Muslim Egypt and Rhodes was more than ever isolated and vulnerable. In 1435 the warlike Egyptian sultan Baybars planned an invasion of Rhodes, and the Knights brought reinforcements in from Europe at full speed, but the threat came to nothing. In 1444 the Egyptians tried again, mounting an invasion of the island and a month-long siege of the town of Rhodes.

In 1480 Ottoman sultan Mehmet II 'the Conqueror' launched a major attack on Rhodes – ostensibly because Muslims on the islands had reported being persecuted, but really as part of military expansion towards southern Italy. A vast Ottoman fleet, reputedly carrying 70,000–100,000 men, appeared off Rhodes in May. It was commanded by Palaeologos Pasha.

On the island, the garrison, under the command of Grand Master Pierre d'Aubusson, had just received reinforcements of around 2,000 foot soldiers and 500 knights from France. D'Aubusson had been vigilant and had prepared well against possible attack, laying in substantial supplies and military equipment.

The Ottomans settled in to a siege. Coming under attack from the citadel, where the garrison was ensconced, the Ottomans launched an assault: they succeeded in building a bridge from the boats in the harbour to the citadel walls but as their men began to pour across it to attack, this makeshift structure collapsed and thousands were drowned in the ensuing panic. A second attack was more successful and some of the Ottoman troops succeeded in raising the sultan's standard on the walls.

HEAVENLY ARMY

Accounts differ as to what happened next. According to the version given by Flemish writer Guillaume Caoursin, the Ottomans were terrified by a vision of the Virgin Mary and a saintly army in the sky above the citadel. Caoursin reports that the Knights had raised banners showing Christ, the Virgin Mary and St John the

Baptist on the walls of the citadel, but that when the Ottoman attack was at its height a golden cross appeared in the clear sky above these banners, together with a miraculous image of the Virgin Mary carrying a spear and a shield and next to her a man in simple clothing standing before a great host of warriors of light. The Ottomans were paralyzed with fear and the Hospitallers were able to cut them down and drive them back.

The Ottoman account, however, suggests that their soldiers were poised for victory when their commander issued the order that there was to be no looting since the wealth of the citadel, and the merchants in the town, belonged to the sultan. This apparently caused the Ottoman warriors to stop fighting and many were slain in their moment of wavering.

OTRANTO PUNISHED

In the wake of this defeat, the Ottoman fleet lifted the siege of Rhodes and sailed away on 28 July 1480. On the island, the merchants, farmers and knights of the Hospitaller garrison rejoiced at their delivery by a seeming miracle from a force of such size. The Ottomans, for their part, sailed on and wreaked a terrible vengeance for the frustration at Rhodes on the people of Otranto in Italy. Having overrun the port, they killed Archbishop Stefano Agricoli in the cathedral and slaughtered 800 citizens of the town who refused to convert to Islam.

▼ *The Ottoman forces preparing for battle outside the walls of Rhodes in 1480. Their attack failed, reputedly after an appearance by the Virgin Mary.*

SULEYMAN TAKES RHODES

BUT THE HOSPITALLERS HOLD MALTA

In 1522, the Hospitaller garrison on Rhodes was forced to surrender after a six-month siege by Ottoman sultan Suleyman I 'the Magnificent' and his army. The Hospitallers departed Rhodes to take up residence on Malta.

PREPARATIONS FOR THE SIEGE

Philippe of L'Isle-Adam was elected Grand Master of the order in 1521 and began at once to prepare for the defence of Rhodes. He sent out an appeal throughout Europe for reinforcements to defend this outpost of Christendom, but received no response save a small contingent from Venice and Crete. He laid in a year of provisions and organized the defence of the town's reconstructed walls and bastions with most particular care, assigning the protection of different areas to groups of knights.

▼ *The Hospitallers had a powerful fleet and were a force to be reckoned with at sea.*

The Ottoman fleet arrived on 26 June under the command of Mustafa Pasha; Sultan Suleyman sailed in around a month afterwards to take command. The Turks launched a concerted assault on a section of the town walls defended by knights of Aragon and England, using both artillery and the digging of mines. This went on for as much as a month, with little progress, but on 4 September the Ottoman attack opened a breach almost 40ft (12m) across beside the bastion of England. The Ottomans gained control of this area, but then a fearless Hospitaller assault led by English knight Nicholas Hussey managed to force the Turks back.

GENERAL ATTACK

On 24 September the Turks mounted a general assault on the town, with particular concentration of fire against the bastions of England, Italy, Provence and Spain. Twice in one day the bastion of

Spain was captured by the Ottomans and then retaken by the Hospitallers. After hours of fierce fighting, with the garrison's powerful cannon killing vast numbers of Ottoman warriors, the attack was at last called off. Suleyman was enraged and ordered the execution of Mustafa Pasha because he had failed to take the city despite his vast numerical advantage; the sultan was persuaded to spare Mustafa, but he replaced him with Ahmed Pasha.

The Ottomans launched another powerful attack in late November, but it was driven back once more. However, the Knights and the townspeople of Rhodes were close to exhaustion and by mid-December were ready to negotiate terms of peace. A truce was called on 11–13 December, but when the townspeople asked for further reassurances regarding their safety, Suleyman ordered the artillery attacks to begin again. His troops took the bastion of Spain on 17 December – and from this point on there seemed no doubt the city would eventually be taken.

PEACE AT LAST

On 20 December Grand Master of L'Isle-Adam requested another truce and on 22 December a peace treaty was agreed under which the Knights who wished to depart would be allowed 12 days to leave the island in peace, with their weapons and religious relics, while the islanders would be permitted to leave for up to three years. Suleyman was very impressed with the fight put up by the Knights and the bearing of Grand Master of L'Isle-Adam. After the peace negotiations, the sultan is reported to have said of of L'Isle-Adam 'it gives me no pleasure to force this fearless old man from his home' and when he entered Rhodes he dismissed his imperial bodyguard, declaring that he had his safety guaranteed on the honour of the Grand Master of the Hospitallers, and that this was 'worth more than all the world's

armies'. A further tribute to the heroism and faith of the Hospitallers came from Holy Roman Emperor Charles V, who declared: 'Nothing in the world was ever so well lost as Rhodes.'

IN MALTA

After leaving Rhodes, the Knights Hospitaller took up residence in Sicily, but in 1530 moved on to Malta, which was given them as a fief, along with the nearby island of Gozo and the port of Tripoli in north Africa, by Holy Roman Emperor Charles V (r.1519–56). In return, they were required to send one falcon a year to the Viceroy of Sicily and to celebrate Mass for Charles on All Saints Day.

From their new base they launched regular attacks on Muslim shipping, and fought a running war against the Muslim corsairs who operated from north Africa across the Mediterranean. In 1551 the corsair Turgut Reis and the Ottoman admiral Sinan combined in an attack on Malta: they did not take the main island, but captured Gozo and, also during the same campaign, drove the Hospitaller garrison from Tripoli. In response the Knights greatly expanded and strengthened fortifications on Malta. In 1559, the Knights took part in an expedition organized by

▼ *Jean Parisot of Valette masterminded the defence of Malta. He was a veteran of the Hospitallers' campaigns in Rhodes.*

Philip II of Spain to drive Turgut Reis from Tripoli. It was a significant enterprise – involving more than 50 galleys and 14,000 men – but ended in a heavy defeat in the Battle of Djerba in May 1560.

THE ASSAULT ON MALTA

Nevertheless, the Hospitallers kept up their attacks on Muslim shipping, and in 1565 Suleyman determined to stop them once and for all. A vast Ottoman war-fleet landed a force of around 40,000–50,000 men on Malta in mid-May. Grand Master Jean Parisot of Valette had sent out a summons to members of the order around the world, but even so its defending garrison numbered no more than around 6,000. He further strengthened the fortifications on the three main forts of Malta – St Elmo, Fort St Michael and Fort St Angelo.

The Ottomans could not use the mining that had worked so well on Rhodes because the fortresses on Malta were built on solid rock. Instead they relied on their mighty artillery, training their guns on the fortress of St Elmo at the entrance to the Grand Harbour. The Ottomans launched three major attacks on St Elmo, on 3, 10 and 16 June, and each time were driven back by the determined defenders; the attackers suffered very heavy losses, and many of the elite Janissary troops were killed. But finally on 23 June, in another major attack, the entire defending garrison of that fort was killed – even the

▲ *In the defence of Malta the Hospitallers fought with heroic courage.*

wounded men who had fought heroically to the last, sitting on chairs on the ramparts. The fort was taken.

Next the Turks attacked the Senglea Peninsula to the south of Fort St Angelo. There was fierce fighting over several days in early August, but the Ottomans were driven back. Another attack on Fort St Michael and the town of Birgu on 7 August seemed to have brought the Turks close to victory when they made a breach in the walls, but they had to retreat to defend their camp against a daring attack by Hospitaller cavalry from Mdina.

THE OTTOMANS DEPART

Further attacks on Fort St Michael and on Mdina also failed and in early September the Ottomans abandoned the attack when a relief force arrived from Sicily. The holding of Malta against seemingly impossible odds was an extraordinary and famous victory that ranked alongside any of the Hospitallers' other feats.

The Knights Hospitaller continued to fight for Christendom at sea and in land wars in eastern Europe and on Crete. They were to remain on Malta until 1798, when they were finally driven out by French general Napoleon en route to Egypt, on the expedition that was to discover the Rosetta Stone.

KNIGHTS OF THE TEMPLE OF SOLOMON
FOUNDATION OF THE KNIGHTS TEMPLAR

The military brotherhood of the Knights Templar was founded in the aftermath of the First Crusade, initially for the care of Christian pilgrims travelling to Jerusalem. The order received the official blessing of the Church at the Council of Troyes in 1129 and this was confirmed and many privileges granted to the order by Pope Innocent II in 1139.

French knights Hugues of Payens and Godfrey of Saint-Omer, both veterans of the First Crusade, took on the responsibility of protecting pilgrims on the road between the port of Jaffa and the Holy City, and in c.1120 proposed the formation of a religious brotherhood to perform this task. King Baldwin II of Jerusalem gave them his backing and provided space for a headquarters in the former al-Aqsa mosque on Temple Mount. At the time, this building was believed to stand on the ruins of the biblical Temple of Solomon and the brotherhood took the name of the 'Poor Knights of Christ and the Temple of Solomon'. Initially there were nine knights in the brotherhood and they had very few resources; their emblem, which shows two

▼ *With the backing of Bernard of Clairvaux, the Templars received the ceremonial blessing of the Roman Catholic Church at the Council of Troyes in 1129.*

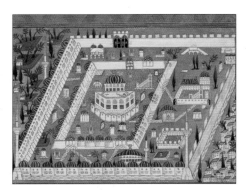

▲ *In crusader Jerusalem the al-Aqsa mosque was used as a palace. The Knights Templar were given space in one wing.*

knights mounted on a single horse, reflects their poverty-stricken beginnings. They took vows of poverty, chastity and obedience and agreed to share all their property.

BERNARD OF CLAIRVAUX
In 1126 Hugues of Payens, by now known as *Magister militum Templi* (Master of the Temple Soldiery) travelled to Europe to raise finances and seek Church support. He had a powerful ally in the Cistercian monk Bernard of Clairvaux, founder and first abbot of the Cistercian Abbey of Clairvaux in north-eastern France, who was also nephew to Andre of Montbard, one of the initial members of the brotherhood. Bernard wrote a pamphlet called *De Laude Novae Militiae* (In Praise of the New Soldiery), in which he set up the Templar knights as ideal exemplars of chivalry and contrasted their Christian poverty and religious devotion with the lack of these qualities in the secular knights of the day, men who expended their God-given energy in private quarrels driven by greed.

The pamphlet took up the imagery used by St Paul in his *Epistle to the Ephesians*, which urged readers to put on 'the whole armour of God' and 'the breastplate of righteousness', to use 'the shield of faith' and 'the helmet of salvation' and fight with 'the sword of the spirit'. Bernard

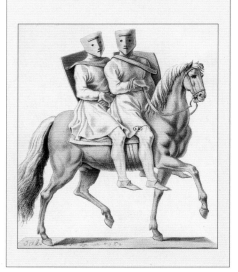

wrote of the new 'fearless knight, secure in every direction, who dons the breastplate of faith to protect his soul just as he dons an iron breastplate on his body'; he added that with this 'double armour' knights need fear nothing, and urged them to go forward in safety, with undaunted spirits, to fight back those who oppose the Cross of Christ.

Hugues of Payens, almost certainly with Bernard's help, drew up a rule for the new order, which was to be committed to protecting pilgrims and the holy places in Jerusalem, and this was approved at the Council of Troyes in January 1129. Five Templars, led by Hugues of Payens, attended the council and received the rule from Bernard. The rule was based on that of the Cistercians.

On his trip of 1128–29, Hugues of Payens also visited England and Scotland, where he established the first Templar house in London and also one close to Edinburgh on land granted to the order by King David I at Balantrodoch (now known as Temple, in Midlothian).

ROBERT OF CRAON

Hugues of Payens died in 1136 and was succeeded as Grand Master by Robert of Craon. Robert won papal approval for the order in 1139. In his bull *Omne Datum Optimum*, Pope Innocent II confirmed the order's rule and granted the Templars exemption from local laws and taxation and also from all secular and religious authority save that of the papacy. He wrote: 'since your religious order and your

▼ *The Templars meet, with great ceremony, in Paris in April 1147, shortly after they were granted privileges by the Church.*

ancient institution is praised throughout the whole world ... you should be regarded especially as part of God's knighthood.' By this date, the order was well established, having already received several substantial gifts of land and finance from the nobility of Europe, many as a result of Bernard of Clairvaux's tract in praise of the order.

The Templars gained further significant privileges in the papal bulls *Milites Templi* of 1144 (issued by Pope Celestine II, who ruled 1143–44) and *Militia Dei* of 1145 (issued by Pope Eugenius III, who ruled 1145–53), which permitted them to build

▲ *Burgundian nobleman Jacques of Molay is inagurated into the Knights Templar. He became Grand Master in 1292, and was also the last Grand Master, for the order was accused of heresy and dissolved in 1312 under his leadership.*

their own places of worship, to bury their dead in the grounds of these establishments and to gather taxes on Templar property once each year. In 1147 Eugenius III granted the knights to right to wear a red splayed cross (one with spreading ends) on their white surplice. The sacred design was sewn above the heart.

ORGANIZATION

The head of the order was the Grand Master. Major decisions were taken by the Grand Chapter, a council of leading officers. Only the Grand Chapter could agree treaties or declare war. Its officers included the Marshal, in charge of military affairs, and the Seneschal, in control of administration, plus eight provincial masters in Aragon, Apulia, England, France, Poitiers, Hungary, Portugal and Scotland.

KNIGHTS TEMPLAR IN THE FIELD

BRAVE BUT OFTEN RECKLESS

The Knights Templar were famed for their bravery and martial prowess – as exemplified by the extraordinary heroism of Jakelin de Mailly, who fought until he was the last knight standing at the Battle of Cresson (1187). However, as a self-contained unit within crusader armies they often fought for the glory of the order above all other considerations. Within the order discipline was extremely strict – and this made the Templars a formidable fighting unit; but in a campaigning army they often undermined overall discipline by acting on their own initiative, seeking their own glory at the expense of strategy.

AT ASCALON

One celebrated example occurred during King Baldwin III of Jerusalem's siege of Ascalon (modern Ashkelon in Israel) in 1153. Baldwin brought a vast army, including the Templars and Hospitallers

▼ *Jakelin of Mailly, who reputedly fought on single-handedly when overwhelmed by Ayyubid troops at Cresson (1187) was the paragon of Templar bravery in battle.*

and all the great barons of the Kingdom of Jerusalem, as well as a contingent of pilgrims and Patriarch Fulcher of Jerusalem carrying a piece of the True Cross; but the city was well garrisoned and supplied with food to endure a long siege. Thus, it was particularly galling that when chance (or some might say the hand of God) gave the crusaders an opportunity, the self-interest of the Templars worked directly against the crusader army's long-term interests.

The Egyptian garrison attempted to burn down one of the crusaders' siege towers but the wind blew the flames back on the city defences and started a conflagration that made a section of the wall collapse. This part happened to be the one assigned to the Templars to attack. The Templars' Grand Master, Bernard of Tremblay, led an assault with 40 of his elite knights but did not tell King Baldwin. He even mounted a guard to prevent other crusaders joining the assault. Some accounts suggest that this was because the Templars wanted to have the glory all for themselves; according to chronicler William of Tyre, Bernard wanted to have

the spoils of the city to enrich the order's coffers. In the event, the 40 knights were overwhelmed by the garrison, the breach was repaired and the crusader army lost its advantage. The heads of Bernard and the Templar knights were displayed on the city walls.

AT AL-MANSOURAH

Another often cited example of Templar rashness in conflict was at the Battle of al-Mansourah during the Seventh Crusade when, following success in a surprise attack on the enemy camp, the Templars and members of other brotherhoods swept into the town of al-Mansourah against the orders of crusade leader King Louis IX of France. Their attack was a failure and jeopardized the entire campaign. All but five Templar knights were killed.

AT HATTIN

The Templar leadership also played a significant – and disastrous – role in the events leading up to the cataclysmic crusader defeat at the Battle of the Horns of Hattin in July 1187. Following Saladin's attack on 2 July on the Castle of Tiberias, King Guy of Jerusalem encamped with a vast army at Sephoria, around 18 miles (29km) away from the castle; initially Guy and his military council were minded to attack Saladin, but Sephoria was a strong defensive position and Count Raymond of Tripoli, who was master of Tiberias and knew the land, urged caution. Raymond insisted that even if he were to lose his castle, and his wife who was within it, he would prefer this outcome to putting the entire Kingdom of Jerusalem at risk by launching an ill-timed and ill-advised assault in difficult terrain.

The council accepted his advice, but that night Templar Grand Master Gerard of Ridefort managed to persuade King Guy to launch an assault on Saladin's army – by convincing him that Raymond was a traitor who had agreed a secret deal with Saladin. The army made a reckless advance, was surrounded by Saladin's troops, and suffered a devastating defeat. The relic of the True Cross was captured and the military strength of the Kingdom of Jerusalem was annihilated.

THE MIGHT OF THE CROSS

At the Horns of Hattin – as at the Battle of Cresson shortly beforehand – Gerard placed his confidence in the might of the cross and showed himself willing to risk all in order to win glory. The Templars and other warrior brotherhoods took pride in waging war by the sword against the armies of Islam and had no time for the methods of negotiation and diplomacy that were increasingly favoured by the lords of the Kingdom of Jerusalem.

In 1148 at the Council of Acre, Templar Grand Master Robert of Craon was one of the voices urging an attack on Damascus while local lords argued rather for building an alliance with Mu'in ad-Din Unur, emir of Damascus, against the Zengid lords of Syria, notably the formidable Nur ed-Din of Aleppo: the resulting siege of

▼ *In 1299 Templar Grand Master, Jacques of Molay, fought the Mamluks in Armenia.*

▲ *The Templar chapel at Cressac, south of Angouleme, France, is decorated with scenes of the Templars fighting in Syria.*

Damascus was a disaster and brought the Second Crusade to a miserable end. In 1172, similarly, the Templars refused to back an alliance between King Amalric of Jerusalem and the Muslim Assassin sect against Nur ed-Din: they were annoyed that the proposed alliance would damage their income, for Templar taxes on Assassin villages were to be waived, and a body of Templar knights murdered a group of Assassins shouting 'No diplomacy with the infidel!' Their action effectively scuppered the deal. According to one chronicler, King Amalric was so angry that he declared his intention to ask the pope to dissolve the Templar order.

In the later crusades in Egypt, the Templars were likewise among those who refused to enter negotiations for the return of Jerusalem on the grounds that the Holy City must be won by the sword and the Christian knights must not negotiate with those of Islam. On the Fifth Crusade the Templars backed the papal legate Pelagius against King John of Jerusalem and the barons of his kingdom when Pelagius turned down the offer of Sultan al-Kamil in Egypt to give possession of Jerusalem and the entire Kingdom of Jerusalem as it

had been before the Battle of the Horns of Hattin if they would return Damietta and leave Egypt.

BROTHERS AT WAR

Such was the rivalry between Templars and Hospitallers over glory and resources that they became effectively enemies on sight. In the 13th century a Templar would draw his sword when he encountered a Hospitaller in the streets; in 1242, the two orders were actually drawn into a sword battle in the streets of Acre. In this period the Templars and Hospitallers secretly worked against one another in their dealings with the enemy.

BRAVERY AT ACRE

In 1291 in the siege of Acre, the last great military engagement of the Kingdom of Jerusalem, the Templars were defending the northern part of the city walls and showed all the bravery and indomitable fighting spirit of old. The Grand Master, William of Beaujeu, gave his life in the struggle at the walls and even after the city fell on 18 May the Templars carried on the fight for a full ten days from their headquarters within the city. By the time they were finally overrun by the invading army, attacks had reduced the Templar palace in Acre to a ruin, and it collapsed, killing defenders and attackers alike.

TEMPLAR BUILDERS

CASTLES AND CHURCHES

The Templars were involved in building from the first years of the brotherhood. When King Baldwin II of Jerusalem gave the founding Templars the Temple Mount as their headquarters in c.1120 he allowed them to develop the area as they pleased. In 1139 a key privilege granted to the order was the freedom to build their own churches and graveyards. In the early-to-mid 12th century they began to build castles to help in the protection of pilgrims and Christian sacred sites in Outremer.

TEMPLAR CASTLES

On the road to Jerusalem from Jaffa, the Templars manned the Castle of Castrum Arnaldi, first erected by the Patriarch and citizens of Jerusalem in c.1130 but subsequently given to the knights. Protecting the southern route to Jerusalem they had the Castle of Le Toron des Chevaliers, or Latrûn: built by Count Rodrigo Gonzalez of Toledo in Spain in 1137–41, during an armed pilgrimage to the Holy Land, and then given to the Templars. Midway between Jerusalem and Jericho, the Templars built a castle at Cisterna Rubea, complemented by a tower close to Jericho.

▼ The Keep of the imposing Templar castle of Chastel Blanc at Safita (north-westen Syria) has walls 9 feet (3 metres) thick.

▲ The impressive five-towered Monzon Castle, on a hilltop in Aragon (in northern Spain), was given to the Templars in 1143.

The Templars were responsible for protecting the mountains to the north of Antioch, the area known as the Amanus March, and they built or garrisoned a number of impressive castles in the region. These included the Castle of Gaston (now known as Baghras), which the Templars manned from c.1154. They lost it to Saladin on 26 September 1188 and he dismantled the fortress, but the Templars regained the repaired castle in 1216. Shortly afterwards, however, they burned it when they had to retreat from the army of Egyptian sultan Baybars.

In Galilee the Templars themselves built the Castle of La Fève before 1172 and perhaps a good deal earlier. When this fortress was captured by Saladin in 1187, it was praised by an Islamic chronicler as 'the finest castle and most strongly fortified, the best supplied with men and munitions … for the Templars this was a powerful castle, a place of refuge and a pillar of strength'. He added that it had a fine pasture and a fountain, and was regularly used by the Templars as a meeting place and a pasture for their horses. We know that the Castle of La Fève was used as a base for armies on campaign. From La Fève, Templar knights under the command of Gerard of Ridefort rode to defeat at the Battle of Cresson.

The Templars also manned the fortress of Gaza, originally built by King Baldwin III of Jerusalem, who gave it to the knights in 1149 as a base for raids against the Muslim garrison in Ascalon and to protect the Kingdom of Jerusalem's southern frontier against attacks from Muslim Egypt. At a crossing of the upper River Jordan, the Templars began building the formidable

▼ The Templars built fortifications in Europe as well as in the Holy Land. Their vast castle at Ponferrada in the kingdom of Léon was constructed in c.1290.

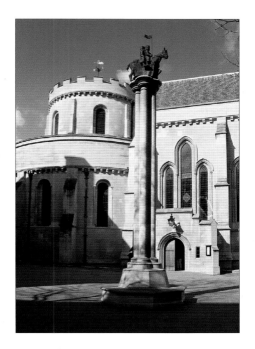

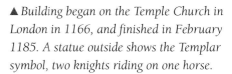

▲ *Building began on the Temple Church in London in 1166, and finished in February 1185. A statue outside shows the Templar symbol, two knights riding on one horse.*

▲ *The imposing Convent of Christ in Tomar, Portugal, was built by Gualdim Pais, provincial master of the order, in 1160. The Templars were fighting against the Moors.*

Castle of Le Chastellet or Jacob's Ford. The position of the castle was a potential threat to Saladin because it guarded the only crossing of the Jordan and the way necessarily taken from Saladin's territory to the Kingdom of Jerusalem; the sultan offered King Baldwin IV a bribe of 100,000 dinars to tear the castle down and when he was refused he prepared to attack. The castle was still unfinished when the attack came in August 1169 and Saladin's sappers were able to bring the incomplete outer wall down. His men poured through the tun-

nel they had excavated and killed 800 of the garrison. Another 700 Templars were executed by Saladin. He dismantled the remains of the castle before he left.

TEMPLAR CHURCHES

The Templars understood that the former al-Aqsa mosque, which they had made their Jerusalem headquarters, was built on the remains of the Temple of Solomon, and they called it the *Templum Solomonis* (Temple of Solomon) or *Templum Domini* (Temple of the Lord). The temple itself, or

perhaps the Church of the Holy Sepulchre in Jerusalem, was the inspiration for a number of Templar churches with round naves in Europe.

These included the Church of the Holy Sepulchre, or 'Round Church', in Cambridge, England, built in 1130, and the Templars' own London headquarters, Temple Church in central London. Originally this building was lavishly decorated within; it was the order's second London base, built when the brotherhood moved from a smaller headquarters in High Holborn, also in central London, and it had a very grand consecration service performed by no less a figure than Patriarch Heraclius of Jerusalem on 10 February 1185, probably in the presence of King Henry II.

The Templars did not build only round churches – the chapel at their castle of Chastel Pelerin (built *c.*1218), now in Israel, had 12 sides and that at Safad Castle (built 1240–60) also had many sides; nor were the Templars the only creators of round churches – the Knights Hospitaller also built chapels and churches in this form. The majority of Templar churches, moreover, are rectangular and undecorated, in line with Bernard of Clairvaux's call for simple architecture.

TEMPLAR BANKERS

The Templars pioneered many methods of banking still in use today. Because the Templars received lavish gifts and had privileges exempting them from taxation, they grew immensely rich and became established as money lenders, providing funds for many monarchs and the Church to finance cathedral building. They used their network of monastic houses, or preceptories, to facilitate the safe transfer of funds for merchants: funds could be paid in at one Templar preceptory, and the credit note issued could be cashed at another preceptory halfway around the world. Money lending or usury was forbidden for Christians, so Templars did not call the fees they charged 'interest' – instead they compared the activity to being a landlord and called the charge 'rent'.

DOWNFALL OF THE TEMPLARS
ACCUSED OF HERESY AND DISBANDED

In the early 14th century the Templars came under a fierce and sustained attack on charges of heresy, pressed particularly by King Philip IV of France (r.1285–1314). The order was dissolved by papal bull *Vox in excelso* of 1312, issued by Pope Clement V (ruled 1305–14).

After the fall of Acre in 1291 the military monastic orders faced an uncertain and difficult future: with no possessions to defend in the Holy Land, their purpose was unclear; the Teutonic Knights and the Hospitallers established monastic states, in Prussia and Rhodes respectively, but the Templars did not. The Templars also faced criticism for the lavish lifestyle of some members, funded by wealth generated from banking and property; they were also subject to attack because many people were in debt to them.

▼ *After executing Jacques of Molay in early 1314, Philip ruled for only a few months. He met an untimely death, mauled by a boar while out hunting in November 1314.*

▲ *Arrested at dawn. Grand Master Jacques of Molay and thousands of French Templars are taken into royal custody.*

MERGER PROPOSAL

One popular solution was the merger of the Templars and the Hospitallers. This proposal was made by, among others, Norman lawyer and pamphleteer Pierre Dubois and by Majorcan novelist, poet and author on chivalry Ramon Llull. King Philip IV of France was strongly in favour, seeing an opportunity to escape his very substantial debts to the Templars, and he proposed that the kings of France should become hereditary masters of a combined order; under this plan, Philip was to lead the knights of the combined order on a new crusade to recover the Holy Land.

In 1305 Bertrand of Goth, Archbishop of Bordeaux, was elected Pope Clement V. He was strongly under the influence of King Philip IV of France, and he established the papal curia not in Rome but in France, first at Poitiers and then, from 1309, at Avignon. In 1306 Clement summoned the two Grand Masters, Jacques of Molay of the Templars and Fulk of Villaret of the Hospitallers, to Poitiers to consider the merger; Jacques arrived in 1307 but Fulk was delayed. Clement raised the

matter with the Templar Master and also discussed accusations of heresy against the Templars that had been made by former Templar knights Esquin of Floyan, Bernard Pelet and Gérard of Byzol. It would appear that Clement was convinced that the charges were false, but he asked Philip IV to investigate.

ON TRIAL

Philip IV saw an opportunity to bring about the downfall of the Templars, cancel his vast debts, and engineer the merger of the monastic orders that he favoured. Philip issued secret orders and in dawn raids on Friday 13 October 1307, 5,000 Templars in France, including Jacques of

---

TEMPLARS IN AMERICA

Some rather fanciful accounts suggest that Knights Templar were in fact the first Europeans to sail to the New World of North America (after the Vikings in *c.*1000). The theory goes that the Templars sailed from Scotland (or perhaps from their port of La Rochelle in western France) after the downfall of the order and settled in Nova Scotia (Latin for 'New Scotland') in 1398, and then moved on to New England in 1399 – almost a century before the voyages of Christopher Columbus, the Genoan explorer usually credited with discovering America. There are gravestones in Nova Scotia that bear crusader crosses, and a hand-cut gravestone in Westford, Massachusetts, is marked with Templar imagery. The Templar Rossyln Chapel in Scotland is reportedly decorated with carvings in stone of American plants such as the *aloe vera*; the chapel was completed in 1486, six years before Columbus's first voyage in 1492.

Molay, were arrested on charges of heresy, blasphemy and sodomy. The accusations centred on the Templars' secret initiation ceremony: it was alleged that an initiate was required to spit on the cross, to deny Christ three times and to kiss the officer who admitted him. There were also claims that initiates worshipped a pagan idol and that knights were not permitted to refuse to have sexual relations with one another. Most Templars admitted to these or similar charges under severe torture.

On 22 November Clement called on all Christian rulers to arrest Templars and to take possession of their assets. He also commanded the French Templars to be released from imprisonment and be given into the care of papal commissioners. In hearings before a papal committee beginning on 24 December 1307 Jacques of Molay and other senior Templars retracted their confessions on the grounds that they had been extracted under torture.

Trials began in 1309 and ran on and off for five years. Before the commission in November 1309 Jacques of Molay declared that he wanted to mount a defence of the order, but had doubts that he could – since he was illiterate and the order did not contain a single lawyer; he

▼ Philip IV used his influence over Pope Clement V to bring about the downfall of the Templars, to whom he was in debt.

▲ The condemned Templars are executed in Paris on 18 March 1314. In 2001 a document uncovered at the Vatican revealed that Pope Clement had secretly absolved Jacques and other Templars in 1308.

put his faith in the pope and seems to have believed, perhaps with the confidence of the innocent, that he and his men would be cleared in the end. Under questioning he declared that the Templars had always been generous in charitable donations, that Templar liturgy was more beautiful than that in any other churches, and that in no other order had the knights shed their blood more readily in defence of the cross of Christ.

One accusation against the Templars that was most widely confessed was that they spat on the cross and denied Christ during their initiation ceremonies. Some historians suggest that this claim may have been true, and was perhaps required as a demonstration of the initiate's total loyalty to the order – overriding all other claims, even that of religious faith.

At the Council of Vienne in 1312 Pope Clement issued the bull *Vox in excelso*, dissolving the Templars, and a second bull, *Ad Providam*, transferring most of the Templars' assets to the Knights Hospitaller. However, a paper found in Vatican archives in 2001 suggests that privately Clement absolved Jacques of Molay, the Templar order and all its knights of guilt.

JACQUES OF MOLAY EXECUTED

On 18 March 1314 at a trial hearing in Paris, Jacques of Molay and leading templar Geoffrey of Charney, Preceptor of Normandy, publicly withdrew their confessions once more and were sentenced to death as relapsed heretics by burning at the stake in central Paris. On his own insistence, Molay was tied facing the cathedral of Notre Dame, and with his hands raised in prayer; legend recounts that at his death he declared that Pope Clement and King Philip would soon meet him before the throne of God. Both men were indeed dead by the end of the year.

Of the remaining Templars some joined the Knights Hospitaller; others probably quietly returned to the secular world. Still others fled beyond the reach of papal power – to Switzerland or to Scotland, which had been excommunicated; some, perhaps, sailed to America (*see* box). In Portugal, the Templars carried on as the Knights of Christ, and in Spain as knights of the Order of Montesa.

▼ Rosslyn Chapel in Midlothian, Scotland, reputedly has Templar connections and secret coded decorations, but many scholars dispute the link to the Templars.

TEUTONIC KNIGHTS
GERMANIC BROTHERHOOD

The German order of the Teutonic Knights was established in Acre in the late 12th century and granted approval by Pope Celestine III (ruled 1191–98) in 1192. In the 13th century the order established itself in Prussia, initially as part of a crusade against pagans in the region and subsequently against the non-Christian people of central and northern Europe. The order suffered a crushing defeat at the hands of a Polish–Lithuanian force at the Battle of Tannenberg in 1410 and became gradually secularized.

ORIGINS AND FOUNDATION
The earliest origins of the order of the Teutonic Knights lie in a hospital for German pilgrims run in Jerusalem from *c.*1140 by German knights under the overall control of the Knights Hospitaller. It was known as the *Domus Teutonicorum* (House of the Germans). In 1189–90 during the siege of Acre on the Third Crusade, German merchants from Lübeck and Bremen set up a sister German hospital in the crusader camp. After the

▲ *Holy Roman Emperor and sometime King of Jerusalem, Frederick II, seen here receiving a delegation of Arabs in 1230, was a major patron of the Teutonic Knights. His chancellor, Petrus of Vinea, pictured on the left, was a Master of the Order.*

▼ *The Teutonic Knights' Montfort Castle was originally so called from the French for 'strong mountain'. The Knights' name for it, Starkenberg, means the same in German.*

capture of Acre in 1191 the hospital was established as a permanent institution in Acre, known as the Hospital of St Mary of the German House in Jerusalem. Initially a simple monastic brotherhood, as recognized by Pope Celestine III in 1192, it became a military order with the approval of King Amalric II of Jerusalem in 1198.

The Teutonic Order received substantial grants of land from popes Celestine III and Innocent III in the Latin Kingdom of Jerusalem and in Germany, Italy and elsewhere. It was Innocent III who, in 1205, granted the knights the use of their white habits, or surplices, decorated with a black cross. The order based its organization on that of the Knights Templar and its head was known as the Grand Master.

MONTFORT
The order's original base was in Acre, but in 1220 the brotherhood bought the Castle of Montfort, or Starkenberg, to the north-east of the city and on the route between the Mediterranean coast and Jerusalem. From 1229 this was the principal seat of the Teutonic Grand Masters, as well as the home of the order's treasury and archive. In 1266 the Knights repelled an attack by Mamluk sultan Baybars, but when he returned in 1271 the garrison surrendered at the end of a seven-day siege. Baybars for once honoured his promise made during negotiations to allow the knights to leave Montfort with their belongings. They returned to Acre.

IN TRANSYLVANIA
Hermann von Salza, Grand Master of the Teutonic Order in 1210–39, was a close friend of Holy Roman Emperor Frederick II. Under von Salza's leadership, the brotherhood began to transfer its operations from the Holy Land to central Europe.

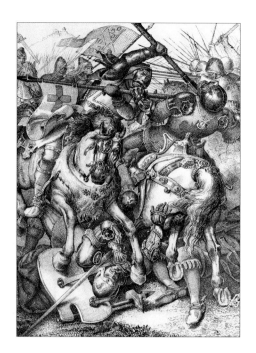

▲ *The Teutonic Knights' days of glory ended when, under Grand Master Ulrich von Jungingen, they were roundly defeated at the First Battle of Tannenberg in July 1410.*

In 1211 the Teutonic Knights entered the service of King Andrew II of Hungary (r. 1205–35) and settled on land he gave them in Burzenland, Transylvania; his aim was to establish a buffer against the border incursions of the nomadic Turkish Cuman people. However, when the Teutonic Knights attempted to establish an independent principality on the territory by appealing to Pope Honorius III (ruled 1216–27) to be placed under his authority rather than that of the Hungarian crown, King Andrew expelled them from the country.

IN PRUSSIA

In 1226 the Teutonic Knights answered a call from Duke Konrad I of Masovia in Poland to fight on his borders against the pagan Prussians who had been provoked to violent uprising by the first Prussian Crusade of 1221. Over 50 years between 1233 and 1283 the knights fought with great ferocity for the conversion of the Prussians. From 1245 the order even had the power to grant crusade indulgences in this struggle without prior papal approval.

The Teutonic Knights governed Prussia as a sovereign 'monastic state' under charters from the Holy Roman Emperor and the papacy. They founded several fortress settlements including Konigsberg (now in the Russian enclave of Kaliningrad Oblast, situated between Poland and Lithuania), Elbing (modern Elblag in northern Poland), Allenstein (modern Olsztyn in north-east Poland) and Memel (modern Klaipeda in Lithuania). But they faced sustained and brutal opposition from pagan Prussians, who (according to the order's chronicles) would 'roast' captured knights in their armour over fires 'like chestnuts'. The order also tried to expand eastwards to convert Russia to Roman Catholicism, but suffered a devastating defeat at the hands of Alexander Nevsky in the Battle of Lake Peipus, 1242.

MARIENBURG

The knights maintained their presence in the Holy Land at Acre but following the fall of that port in 1291 and the final collapse of Outremer, they briefly made their main base in Venice, Italy, from where they planned ways to retake the Holy Land. In 1309, however, they built a vast castle in Prussia named Marienburg (Mary's Castle)

▼ *Teutonic Knights encounter pagan east German farmers during their attempts to impose Christianity in the region.*

in honour of the Virgin Mary. This place (now Malbork in Poland) was thereafter their main base. In the 14th century they waged a long war against pagans in the Baltic, in the area known as Livonia (now Lithuania, Latvia and Estonia).

The knights were also engaged in wars against Poland, because their expansion cut the country off from its access to the Baltic Sea, and with Lithuania even after that country's conversion to Christianity in 1387. In 1410 Poland and Lithuania joined forces and defeated the Teutonic Knights at the Battle of Tannenberg. The brotherhood ceded territory to Poland, and further landholdings in 1466 following defeat by the Poles and the knights' own Prussian vassals in the Thirteen Years War (1454–66). The order survived in East Prussia, but the Grand Master held the land as a vassal of the Polish king.

DECLINE AND REBIRTH

In 1525 Grand Master Albert of Brandenberg dissolved the order and founded a secular duchy in Prussia under his own rule. Gradually over the ensuing 400 years, the order's territories were ceded to secular authorities. In 1809 the French emperor Napoleon dissolved the order entirely and seized its remaining holdings. However, the Teutonic Knights enjoyed a rebirth in Vienna in 1834 as an ecclesiastical body engaged in charitable work.

WARRIORS OF THE SPANISH RECONQUISTA

SPANISH AND PORTUGUESE ORDERS OF KNIGHTHOOD

A number of military brotherhoods were formed in Spain and Portugal as part of the *Reconquista* (Reconquest), the 770-year war waged between 722 and 1492 to win back those countries from Muslim control.

The first Spanish military brotherhoods were formed shortly after the establishment of the Knights Hospitaller and the Knights Templar in 1110–20. In the 1130s a number of Templar foundations were made in Spain, and on his death in 1134 King Alfonso I *El Batallador* (the Warrior) of Aragon and Navarre left the entire kingdom of Aragon to be shared between the Templars and Hospitallers.

The bequest was annulled, and in the event the Templars and Hospitallers took on the care and defence of a number of castles both in Aragon and elsewhere in Spain; however, they were generally not keen to be drawn into the war against Muslims in Spain because their main interest was to use European landholdings to raise money and men to fight for the cross in the Holy Land.

THE ORDER OF CALATRAVA

In 1157 the Templars told King Alfonso VII of León and Castile that for this reason they were abandoning the Castle of Calatrava in southern Castile. At this point

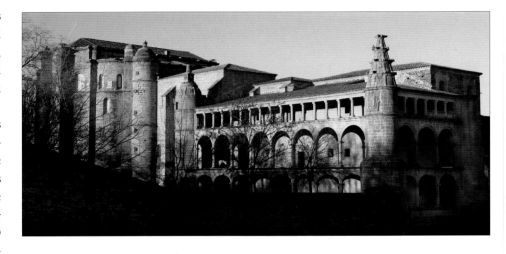

Raymond, Abbot of the Cistercian monastery of Fitero, offered to man and defend the castle with Cistercian lay brothers; he had been persuaded to do so by a former knight turned monk named Diego Valasquez. The monks held Calatrava until Raymond's death in 1163, after which some withdrew to the monastery of Cirvelos. The remainder stayed on, elected Don Garcia as their first Grand Master and established the Order of Calatrava.

The order was recognized as a militia by Pope Alexander III (ruled 1159–81) on 26 September 1164. The brothers' rule,

▼ *The Knights of Calatrava had monastic beginnings, but repeatedly proved their worth in battle against the Moors.*

▲ *King Alfonso IX of the Spanish kingdom of León conquered Alcantara on the River Tagus from the Moors and gave it into the protection of the Knights of Calatrava. The town's imposing Convent of St Benedict was built later, in the 16th century.*

based on that of Cistercian lay brothers, was approved in 1187 by Pope Gregory VIII (pope for less than two months in 1187). It included the requirement that the brothers keep silent when eating and sleeping and sleep in their armour. Unlike the Templars and Hospitallers, the order was subject to secular authority and its Grand Master took an oath of loyalty to the King of Castile.

The Knights of Calatrava had mixed fortunes on the field of battle. Alongside the Castilian army they suffered a heavy defeat at the hands of the Moors at the Battle of Alarcos in 1195 and as a result lost the Castle of Calatrava; the survivors settled in the Cistercian monastery of Cirvelos, and then built a new stronghold at Salvatierra in 1198. They also lost this castle to the Moors in 1209, but in 1212 recaptured Calatrava and then fought in the great Christian victory of that year at the Battle of Las Navas de Tolosa. After which they built a new headquarters, Calatrava La Nueva just 8 miles (12km) from their original home.

▲ *A Spanish nobleman wears the cross of Alcantara on his court clothes. By the 16th century, when this portrait was painted, the knights no longer lived as monks.*

THE ORDER OF ALCANTARA

The knights of the Order of Alcantara, which grew from a brotherhood established in the 12th century in the Kingdom of Leon, came under the protection of the Order of Calatrava in *c.*1218. Its knights were originally called the Knights of St Julian of Pereiro: according to tradition, St Julian was a hermit who inspired a group of knights to build and garrison a castle on the River Tagus. They were known to have existed in 1176 and were recognized by Pope Celestine III in 1197; in 1218 they took over the defence of the Castle of Alcantara from the Order of Calatrava. Like the Calatrava brothers, the Alcantara knights followed the Cistercian rule.

THE ORDER OF AVIZ

The Portuguese knights of the Order of Aviz were also under the protection of the knights of Calatrava. Originally known as the Brothers of Santa Maria of Evora, the Order of Aviz had possession of the town of Evora, taken from the Moors in 1211; they subsequently took possession of the Castle of Aviz and named themselves after it, the Knights of St Benedict of Aviz. They

followed the Benedictine, then the Cistercian rule. The knights of Calatrava passed control of a number of their castles in Portugal to the Order of Aviz.

THE ORDER OF SANTIAGO

Established in *c.*1170, the Order of Santiago had its origins in a brotherhood of knights founded to protect pilgrims travelling to the shrine of Saint James (Santiago) at Compostela. Also known as the Order of Saint James of Compostela, it had it headquarters at Uclés in Castile. It followed the rule of the canons of Saint Augustine. The order was unusual in that, unlike other military orders, from the start the knights of Santiago had the right to marry. In the mid-13th century the knights of Santiago won a great reputation fighting in the campaigns of King Ferdinand III of Castile (reigned 1217–52) against the Moors in southern Spain and they played a notable part in the siege and capture of Seville in 1247–48.

▼ *Knights of the Order of St James of Compostela were granted their first monastic rule in 1171 by Cardinal Jacinto, who later became Pope Celestine III.*

POST-TEMPLAR ORDERS

Following the dissolution of the Knights Templar in 1312, the new Order of Montesa was established in the Kingdom of Aragon by King James II of Aragon. The new order, dedicated to the Virgin Mary, took on the Templar properties in Aragon and Valencia. It was approved by Pope John XXII in 1317. The order was affiliated to the Order of Calatrava. In Portugal the Military Order of Christ was established to take on the property of the Templars. Its brothers were known as Knights of Christ.

OTHER SPANISH ORDERS

The Order of the Knights of Our Lady of Mountjoie was established by Spanish knight Count Rodrigo and received official approval from Pope Alexander III (ruled 1159–81) in 1180. It was named after the hill of Mountjoie, the 'hill of joy' from which the men of the First Crusade first saw Jerusalem. The brothers – all Spaniards – had their headquarters on Mountjoie and also had landholdings in Castile and Aragon and had responsibility for protecting pilgrims there. Their emblem was a red-and-white cross.

The brotherhood had difficulty with recruitment and was renamed the Order of Trufac in 1187. Several of its knights were killed at the disastrous Battle of Hattin in 1187 and the remainder left the Holy Land and settled in Aragon. In 1221 King Ferdinand of Aragon merged it with the Order of Calatrava.

Other Spanish brotherhoods included the Order of Montegaudio, founded in Aragon in *c.*1173; that of Saint George of Alfama, established in *c.*1200; and that of Saint Mary of Spain, created in *c.*1270. The Order of Montegaudio merged with the Knights Templar in 1196. The Order of Saint Mary of Spain combined with the Order of Santiago in 1280. The Order of the Blessed Virgin Mary of Mercy was established in 1218 in Barcelona.

KNIGHTS OF ST THOMAS

THE HOSPITALLERS OF ST THOMAS OF CANTERBURY AT ACRE

The English military brotherhood of the Knights of St Thomas of Canterbury at Acre was established after the capture of the city by crusader armies led by King Richard I of England (r.1189–99) and King Philip II of France (r.1180–1223) in 1191. Some sources suggest its founder was a certain William, chaplain to the Dean of St Paul's Cathedral, London, although there is also evidence that the knights celebrated no less a figure than Richard Coeur de Lion himself as their founder. Their brotherhood was named in honour of Saint Thomas Becket, the Archbishop of Canterbury who had been slain in his own cathedral by English knights in 1170 and canonized in 1173 (*see* box). The order survived for around 340 years, until it was wound up by King Henry VIII of England (r.1509–47) as part of the Dissolution of the Monasteries in 1538.

▼ *The Fifth Crusade was mainly against Ayyubid Egypt, but its initial stages took place in the Holy Land, and at this time Peter Roches established the Knights of St Thomas as a military order.*

CARING FOR THE SICK

In its first years the brotherhood was a religious rather than a military order, dedicated to caring for the wounded and sick, burying the knights who had died in the wars of the cross and seeking to raise funds in order to ransom Christian warriors who had been taken prisoner by Saladin and his Muslim generals. The

◄ *Peter Roches, Bishop of Winchester and the man who transformed the St Thomas brotherhood from monks to knights, founded Titchfield Abbey in Hampshire in c.1222.*

brothers took vows of poverty, chastity and obedience like their counterparts in other monastic orders. In Acre they built a church and a hospital, both dedicated to St Thomas of Canterbury.

The brotherhood was made into a military order by Peter Roches, Bishop of Winchester, when he was in the Holy Land for the Fifth Crusade of 1217–21. He established the brotherhood under the rule of the Teutonic Knights with the backing of the Latin Patriarch of Jerusalem and leading magnates of Outremer. The brotherhood was recognized by Pope Gregory IX (ruled 1227–41) in 1236. The order became more generally known as the Knights of St Thomas Acon (the last word being an anglicized form of Acre). In the first 80 years or so of its existence, the brotherhood had a prior as its senior figure, but from *c*.1279 – reflecting increasing militarization – the pre-eminent individual was the master.

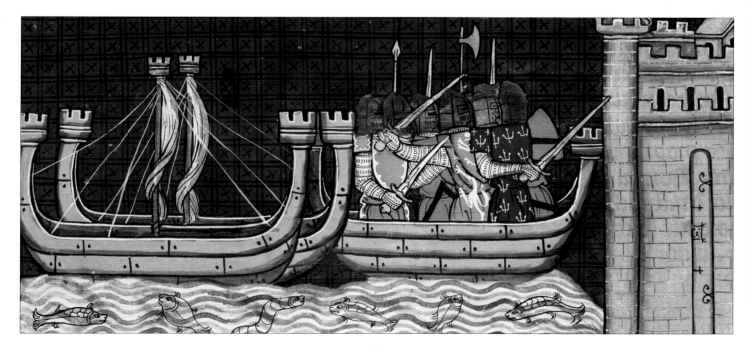

Historians are not certain why members of religious brotherhoods initially dedicated to providing medical and other care for pilgrims and soldiers became themselves soldiers. It is likely that the constant shortage of warriors in Outremer was an important incentive for the brothers to take up arms and further the Christian cause themselves. Bishop Peter Roches would surely have been encouraged in his militarization of the Order of St Thomas of Acre when he sought the counsel of Outremer's leading barons, for these men faced a constant struggle to find enough soldiers to fight their wars and maintain hard-won territories.

The brothers fought in defence of Christian holdings in the Holy Land and, in particular, to protect Acre. They did not become wealthy. In 1279 they were forced to appeal to King Edward I of England (r.1272–1307) for funds. But they did succeed in establishing a house in London and various provincial quarters in both England and Ireland.

▼ *Mercers Hall in Ironmonger Lane, London, stood on the site of the former Hospital of St Thomas Acon, which was destroyed in the Great Fire of London (1666). The hall as shown here was itself destroyed by German bombs in May 1941.*

THE CULT OF ST THOMAS BECKET

King Henry II of England (r.1154–89) elevated Thomas Becket to greatness, making him Chancellor in 1155 and Archbishop of Canterbury in 1162 but the pair quarrelled over Henry's attempts to impose his authority on the Church and, despite an apparent reconciliation, four knights claiming to be acting on Henry's wishes killed Becket in Canterbury Cathedral on 29 December 1170. The whole of Christendom was outraged and in 1173 Pope Alexander III (ruled 1159–81) canonized the archbishop. Becket's cult was immediately very strong and his tomb at Canterbury became a major draw for pilgrims. For his part, Henry II strongly denied having ordered the murder of his archbishop, but was forced to make a public demonstration of penance at the saint's tomb in July 1174.

▲ *Two murderous knights violate the sanctuary at Canterbury Cathedral and slay Thomas Becket at his prayers.*

IN CYPRUS

After the fall of Acre in 1291 the brothers removed, with the Knights Templar, to Cyprus. There they built the fine Church of St Nicholas in Nicosia. But very difficult times followed. In the early 14th century the London house of the Knights of St Thomas was reported to be in ruins and the brothers had to fight off two proposed takeovers, firstly by the Knights Templar and secondly by the convent of Bonhommes at Ashridge, Hertfordshire.

In c.1320 the master of the order in Cyprus, Henry of Bedford, removed to London and established himself in power there. He sent a deputy to rule in Cyprus, but the brothers rejected this man and there was a spilt in the order. Overall power briefly returned to Cyprus after Henry's death, but in c.1360 it was finally confirmed in London; there are no records of a master in Nicosia after this date.

From this period onwards, the brothers appear to have abandoned their military role and exchanged the rule of the Teutonic Knights for that of the monastic rule of the Augustinians. They concentrated on charitable and educational work in London, where they established St Thomas of Acres grammar school in the city in c.1450. The order was dissolved by Henry VIII in 1538 in the Dissolution.

MERCERS

Henry put the brothers' London hospital and chapel up for sale and the buildings were bought by the Worshipful Company of Mercers. Incorporated under royal charter in 1394, the Worshipful Company of Mercers was established as a trade association for merchants in the cloth trade, especially importers of velvet and silk and exporters of wool. The Mercers had already established links with the Knights of St Thomas and had been worshipping in the brotherhood's London chapel for some years. This was destroyed in the Great Fire of London in 1666, but a statue of Christ was salvaged and reused both in the second Mercer's Hall and Chapel (destroyed in World War I) and in its modern replacement.

THE ORDER OF ST LAZARUS

AND OTHER MINOR CHIVALRIC ORDERS

A number of smaller chivalric orders complemented the major brotherhoods of the Knights Templar, the Knights Hospitaller and the Teutonic Knights. Among these, as we have seen, was the brotherhood of the Knights of St Thomas at Acre. Others included the Order of St Lazarus of Jerusalem, established *c*.1123, and the Order of the Sword, founded by King Peter of Cyprus in 1347.

THE ORDER OF ST LAZARUS

Another group of knights in the Holy Land who were dedicated to relieving the suffering of pilgrims and soldiers in the wars of the cross belonged to the Order of St Lazarus of Jerusalem, which specialized in the care of lepers. Like the Order of St John (Hospitallers), St Lazarus grew into a military order from a brotherhood offering hospitality and medical care. Under the Templar rule, any Templar knights who contracted leprosy were required to transfer to the Order of St Lazarus, and

▲ *Henry II of England was an important patron of the Order of St Lazarus. His effigy is at Fontevrault Abbey, France.*

these Templars trained the St Lazarus brothers in military ways. The Order of St Lazarus of Jerusalem was established as a military brotherhood in *c*.1123.

The order became very wealthy, and was left endowments by European kings including Louis VII of France (r.1137–80), Henry II of England (r.1154–89) and Holy Roman Emperor Frederick II (r.1220–50). The order followed the Augustinian rule. Knights of the Order fought at the Battle of La Forbie in 1244 against the alliance of Khwarismian Turks and Sultan as-Salih Ayyub of Egypt (r.1240–49), in the army of the Seventh Crusade led by King Louis IX of France (r.1226–70) and at the fall of Acre in 1291.

The order received papal recognition under Augustinian rule in 1255 in the reign of Pope Alexander IV (ruled 1254–61), and was granted the same privileges and exemptions as the principal monastic orders in 1262 under Pope Urban IV (ruled 1261–64). Its numbers were swelled after 1265 when Pope Clement IV (ruled 1265–68) issued an order that Catholic clergy send all lepers to the houses of St Lazarus.

After the loss of Jerusalem in 1187, the Knights of St Lazarus (like the Hospitaller counterparts) removed to Acre. Then, following the fall of Acre in 1291, the Order

of St Lazarus disappeared from the East altogether while the Hospitallers as we have seen took up residence on Cyprus. The Knights of St Lazarus continued to maintain leper hospitals in Europe.

THE ORDER OF THE SWORD

The future Peter I of Cyprus, the titular King of Jerusalem in 1358–69 and the monarch known as the 'Crusading king', led a military expedition in 1365 against Muslim Egypt. He founded the chivalric brotherhood of the Order of the Sword

▼ *Those afflicted with leprosy, who entered the Order of St Lazarus, were required to pass their worldly goods to the brothers.*

▼ *The Knights of St Lazarus are named after the man raised from the dead by Christ, as told in the Gospel of St John.*

Mary the mother of Christ, was honoured in the brotherhood of Our Lady Of Bethlehem, established to counter the power of the Ottomans in the mid-15th century.

in 1347. In a powerful mystical experience, Peter had a vision of a floating cross and heard a voice urging him to liberate the Holy Land: the order he formed was for knights and men-at-arms prepared to dedicate themselves to freeing Jerusalem and other parts of Outremer from Muslim control. Its emblem was a silver sword, point down, against a blue backing inscribed with the words 'With this maintain loyalty'.

THE ORDER OF OUR LADY OF BETHLEHEM

After the Ottoman Turks under Sultan Mehmed II 'the Conqueror' (r.1444–46, 1451–81) captured Constantinople in 1453, Pope Pius II (ruled 1458–64) established the Order of Our Lady of Bethlehem on the island of Lemnos in the Aegean Sea. Its knights were charged with defending the island against the Ottomans and countering the Turks' activity in the Aegean and Hellespont. The knights of the order wore a white surplice with a red cross and followed a rule similar to that of the Knights Hospitaller.

Pope Pius suppressed a number of orders, including that of St Lazarus, in order to provide the knights of Our Lady of Bethlehem with property and revenues.

But the enterprise came to nothing when the Ottomans succeed in capturing Lemnos. The orders Pius had suppressed were re-established.

OTHER GERMANIC ORDERS

A number of minor Germanic military-monastic orders of knighthood were established in the 13th century. The Order of Dobrzyn, also known as the *Fratres Milites Christi de Prussia*, (the Prussian Cavaliers of Christ Jesus), was created in the 1220s by Christian of Oliva, the first Bishop of Prussia, in order to fight against raids on Masovia by pagan Prussians who had risen in defiance of Duke Konrad I of Masovia's efforts to force them to convert

to Christianity. The establishment of the order was approved by Pope Gregory IX (ruled 1227–41) in 1228. The order was granted possession of the town of Dobrzyn and surrounding regions (Dobrzyn Land). The order initially had 15 German knights in membership under the command of Master Brunon. In 1235 the majority of the knights joined the Teutonic Order.

The monastic order of the Livonian Brothers of the Sword was established by Albert of Buxhoeveden, third Bishop of Riga in Livonia, in 1202 and was granted official sanction by Pope Innocent III in 1204. Bishop Albert wanted the German warrior monks to help in the forcible conversion to Christianity of pagan Curonians, Livonians and others in the region. The knights, who were also known as 'Christ Knights', 'Sword Brethren' and 'The Militia of Christ of Livonia', made their headquarters at Fellin (modern Viljandi in Estonia) and the remains of their Grand Master's castle can still be seen there. They suffered a heavy defeat by Lithuanians at the Battle of Schaulen in 1236 and in 1237 most of the members joined the Teutonic Order.

▼ *Two minor Germanic orders – those of Dobrzyn and of the Livonian Brothers of the Sword – were established by bishops.*

THE EUROPEAN CRUSADES

Christian wars were waged against Muslims in Spain from as early as the 8th century, and against the pagan peoples of northern Europe from the time of the Second Crusade (1147–49) up until the 14th century. In southern France the Albigensian Crusade of the 13th century brutally attacked the Cathars, who were denounced as heretics by the papacy; in Bohemia the Hussites (followers of Czech nationalist preacher Jan Hus) were likewise declared heretics and attacked by crusaders in 1420–32; and in Italy during the 12th–14th centuries, several holy wars were called against enemies of the Catholic Church.

Many of these wars were thinly disguised secular struggles – those in Italy, for example, were fought to promote the territorial interests of the papacy. They were different in kind to the crusades in the Holy Land, and would probably have been fought even if the ideology of crusading was not deployed. One of them, the war to reconquer Spain, predated the crusading era, for it began in the immediate aftermath of the Muslim conquest of the Iberian Peninsula in the early 8th century. Yet, once available, crusading rhetoric and the apparatus of crusade indulgences and taxes were enthusiastically applied to this Spanish struggle from the time of the First Crusade in the 1090s. The call to fight for the cross also gave an added force and charge to all the struggles termed as the Northern Crusades against Muslims, heretics or pagans.

▲ *King Alfonso XI of Castile waged war against Muslims in Spain with such determination he was called 'the Implacable'.*

◄ *After the conquest in 1492 of Granada, the last remaining Muslim territory in Spain, Ferdinand and Isabella receive Arab tributes.*

THE RECONQUISTA
THE STRUGGLE IN SPAIN

◄ *At the Battle of Guadalete (711) in the far south of the Iberian Peninsula, invading Muslim cavalry routed the Visigoths.*

The *Reconquista* – from the word in Spanish and Portuguese for 'reconquest' – was the struggle by the Christians of Europe to retake the Iberian Peninsula from its Moorish rulers. The Reconquista lasted a full 750 years, from the early 8th century, when Muslim Arabs and Berbers captured the peninsula from the Visigoths, to 1492, when the combined armies of Aragon and Castile conquered the city of Granada, the last Muslim territory in the peninsula. These Iberian wars were promoted as holy wars by popes who offered crusading privileges to those taking part in the struggle.

VISIGOTHS AND MUSLIMS
In the 5th century AD the Visigoths, an East Germanic tribe, took power in the Roman province of Hispania (incorporating the whole of the Iberian Peninsula and part of southern France) under the auspices of Rome. After the fall of the Roman Empire in the west, the Visigoth territory became an independent territory.

A Muslim army of Arabs and north African Berber tribesmen invaded the southern part of the peninsula in 711 and in five years captured most of the large Visigoth kingdom. The Muslims then attempted to push on northwards but were defeated by Odo, Duke of Aquitaine, at the Battle of Toulouse in 721 and by Frankish leader Charles Martel in the Battle of Tours in 732. Thereafter they largely abandoned attempts at northward expansion and settled in what is now Spain and Portugal.

Only in the north of the Iberian Peninsula did the Visigoths maintain a foothold. The Visigoth nobleman Pelayo established the Kingdom of Asturias, which was subsequently to be an important base for the reconquest of Spain. His defeat of a Muslim army in the Battle of Covadonga (722) is often identified as the first conflict of the Reconquista.

AL-ANDALUS AND THE MOORS
The Muslim state in the Iberian Peninsula was known by the Arabic name al-Andalus – and its people were known by the Christians as 'Moors'.

Al-Andalus was at first nominally subject to the Umayyad caliph in Damascus, Syria. 'Caliph' was the title for the leader of Islam as a successor to the founder of the faith, the Prophet Mohammad; the Umayyads were the successors of the fourth caliph, Mu'awiyah, a member of the Umayyad clan of caravan merchants.

In 750 the Umayyad caliph Marwan II was defeated by a rival leader, Abu al-Abbas, who established the Abbasid caliphate. Abu al-Abbas was known as *as-Saffah* ('the Bloodshedder') on account of the ruthlessness with which he eliminated his rivals, but one prominent Umayyad, Abd ar-Rahman, escaped to Spain and established himself in Córdoba. His successors were in theory subordinate to the Abbasid caliphs, who were now based in Baghdad, in Iraq, but were in practice independent and ruled as emirs of Córdoba. When Abbasid power declined sharply and their realm fell into anarchy in the early 10th century, the then emir, Abd ar-Rahman III, declared himself the

▼ *The Arabs capture Córdoba. Under their rule it became one of the world's largest cities, home to as many as 500,000 people.*

independent caliph of Córdoba in 929. Historians call al-Andalus the Umayyad caliphate province from 711 to 750, the Emirate of Córdoba fom 750 to 929, and the Caliphate of Córdoba from 929 to 1031. After 1031, the caliphate broke up into small Muslim kingdoms.

ST JAMES THE GREAT

Descendants of King Pelayo of Asturias seized territory in Galicia (the north-west part of the peninsula). In the reign of King Alfonso II of Asturias (r.791–842), the bones of St James were reputedly discovered at Compostela, which became established as one of Europe's foremost pilgrimage sites. St James the Great was one of Christ's 12 Apostles and traditionally brought the Christian Gospel to the Iberian Peninsula. According to legend, his bodily remains were brought to what is now Spain by sea after his death. In 844 the saint then supposedly made a miraculous appearance to lead the Christian army of King Ramiro I of Asturias (r.842–50) against the Moors of Córdoba in the Battle of Clavijo.

PROGRESS IN THE RECONQUISTA

Gerona and Barcelona were taken from the Muslims in 785 and 801 by Carolingian armies from France, and the region of Catalonia became part of the Carolingian realm known as 'the Spanish March'. After 850 the Christian buffer between southern France and the Iberian Peninsula established by the Kings of Asturias was expanded to the valley of the River Duero. In 913 the rulers of Asturias moved their seat of power from Oviedo to León and the kingdom became known as León. Christian kingdoms were also established in Pamplona and Aragon.

In 1002 the caliphate of Córdoba collapsed and divided into around 30 small *taifa* (successor) kingdoms that were to prove vulnerable to the continuing Christian recovery. In 1029 the independent kingdom of Castile was founded in what had been a county within the kingdom of León.

ALFONSO VI AND EL CID

King Alfonso VI of León temporarily reunited his kingdom with Castile, reigning as king of Castile and León from 1072, until his death in 1109. When he captured Toledo in May 1085, he appeared to be on the brink of a major onslaught against the taifa kingdoms: in 1077 he had declared himself Emperor of Spain. But the beleaguered rulers of the taifas appealed to the Muslim Almoravids of north-west Africa, and Almoravid armies defeated Alfonso at Sagrajas in 1086 and Ucles in 1108.

In this period, Don Rodrigo Diaz of Vivar, the Spanish knight celebrated as 'El Cid', performed his great feats of chivalry. He was cast into exile by King Alfonso in 1081, entered the service of al-Mu'tamin, Moorish king of Saragossa, and then fought for al-Mu'tamin and his successor al-Musta'in II for almost ten years, before returning to Alfonso's service and capturing the Muslim kingdom of Valencia in 1090–94; he ruled Valencia until his death in 1099, when it was captured by the Almoravids. (León and Castile remained reunited until 1157.)

▼ *In the legendary Battle of Clavijo, a Christian army was vastly outnumbered by the Moors but triumphed nonetheless after a miraculous appearance by St James.*

CRUSADING PRIVILEGES

War against Muslims in Spain was promoted as crusading, with privileges identical to those offered for military service in the Holy Land, from the 1090s onwards. In 1095 Pope Urban II (ruled 1088–99) urged the Spanish to respond to his call to crusade by fighting the Muslims in their own land rather than by travelling to Palestine. In 1123 Pope Callixtus II (ruled 1119–24) declared a crusade in Spain at the same time as he called a fresh military expedition to the Holy Land.

At the time of the Second Crusade during 1145, Pope Eugenius III (ruled 1145–53) also called a crusade in Spain, guaranteeing King Alfonso VII of León and Castile (r. 1126–57) the same indulgence he had given to the French crusader knights. In 1147 crusader armies from England, Scotland, Normandy and Germany stopped in Spain and Portugal en route to the Holy Land and helped to recapture the city of Lisbon; around the same time, as part of the crusading campaign, Alfonso VII of Castile and Count Ramon Berenguer IV of Barcelona conquered Almeria in south-eastern Spain from the Moors. The next major crusading activity in the Iberian Peninsula was to come in 1212.

THE SPANISH CRUSADE OF 1212

AND OTHER 13TH-CENTURY CRUSADES IN SPAIN AND PORTUGAL

In 1212 Pope Innocent III (ruled 1198–1216) proclaimed a crusade in Spain against the Almohad caliphs. The Almohads had ousted their Almoravid predecessors and defeated the kingdom of Castile in the Battle of Alarcos on 19 July 1195. With the support of troops from the Spanish kingdoms of Aragon and Navarre and with crusaders from France, King Alfonso VIII of Castile (r.1158–1214) won a resounding victory over the Almohads at the Battle of Las Navas de Tolosa, one of the greatest and most important Christian victories in the entire period of the Reconquista.

RISE OF THE ALMOHADS

The Almohads were originally followers of a Berber religious teacher named Ibn Tumart from the Atlas Mountains of

▼ *King Alfonso VIII led the army of Castile and a vast force of crusaders and Knights Templar to victory over the Almohads at the Battle of Las Navas de Tolosa in July 1212.*

Morocco. Ibn Tumart established the Almohads as a religious order dedicated to bringing purity back into the faith of Islam, and after declaring himself the *mahdi* (a promised Islamic redeemer) in 1121, he led armed resistance against the Almoravid caliphs ruling in northern Africa. His successor, Abd al-Mu'min, defeated the Almoravids by 1147 and made himself Emir of Marrakech in 1149; another Almohad leader, Abu Ya'qub Yusuf (r.1163–84), conquered the Almoravid empire in Spain and established a capital in Seville.

Meanwhile King Alfonso VIII of Castile led resistance to the Almohads in Spain. In 1190, following a defeat, Alfonso was forced to agree an armistice, but when this expired in 1194 he attacked the Almohad province of Seville. Almohad caliph Abu Yusuf gathered an army and inflicted a heavy defeat on Alfonso near the fortress of Alarcos, making the Castilian king retreat to Toledo.

In the aftermath of this defeat, the Almohads took a great deal of territory – capturing Trujillo, Talavera, Cuenca, Ucles and the fortress of Calatrava, stronghold of the Spanish monastic military brotherhood the Order of Calatrava. These Muslim successes forced the border between Muslim and Christian Spain many miles northwards, until it lay in the hills just south of Toledo.

Alfonso's ally Rodrigo Jiménez of Rada, Archbishop of Toledo, sought Church backing for a crusading response. Pope Innocent III issued a call to arms, and in 1212 crusaders – including Frankish knights under Archbishop Arnold of Narbonne and members of the military-monastic brotherhood of the Knights Templar – arrived at Toledo. They marched southwards, accompanied by the armies of Aragon, León and Castile. They captured Calatrava, Alarcos and Benevente before they met the Almohad army.

GLORY OF NAVARRE

According to legend, King Sancho VII of Navarre broke into the Almohad caliph's camp at the climax of the Battle of Las Navas de Tolosa. The story goes that the caliph had surrounded his tent with a defensive barrier made of slaves chained together, but that Sancho cut through the barrier and burst into the tent. To celebrate his feat of arms, Navarre changed its coats of arms to one showing a golden chain, below.

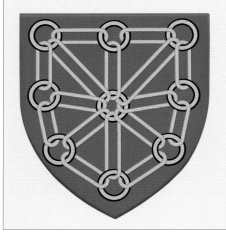

LAS NAVAS DE TOLOSA

The Almohad caliph, Muhammad al-Nasir, gathered his army on the plains of Las Navas de Tolosa. The Christians, trying to reach them though the mountain pass of La Llosa, found it heavily guarded, but then with the help of a local shepherd found a different route through the Despenaperros Pass.

After a prolonged stand-off, the two armies clashed. King Alfonso led the Christian forces into battle, and they won a famous victory – killing, wounding or capturing no fewer than 100,000 of the Almohads at the cost of 2,000 of their own men dead or wounded. Tradition has it that King Sancho VII of Navarre (r.1194–1234) humiliated the Almohad emir in his tent following an act of great

▲ *King Ferdinand III of Castile and León receives homage from a Moor after taking Seville in 1248. The city had been in Moorish hands since its conquest in 712.*

bravery (*see* box). The Almohad caliph, al-Nasir, fled to Marrakech in Morocco, where he died shortly afterwards. Alfonso went on to capture the southern towns of Baeza and Ubeda.

CHRISTIAN TRIUMPHS

In the following years, the victory at Las Navas de Tolosa proved to have been a truly significant one, for the Almohad empire fell apart in dynastic struggles after 1224 and without strong leadership was unable to hold back the armies of the Christian reconquest. King Alfonso IX of León (r.1188–1230) captured Caceres (1227) and Merida and Badajoz (1230), opening the way to the recapturing of Seville. Ferdinand III, who reigned as King of Castile 1217–52 and of León 1230–52, captured Córdoba in 1236), Jaen in 1246 and Seville in 1248. (Ferdinand is celebrated as San Fernando after he was canonized on 4 February 1671.)

King Alfonso X of Castile and León (r.1252–84) defeated the Muslim emirates in Niebla and Murcia. (Alfonso was the father of Eleanor of Castile, beloved wife of King Edward I of England, and it was at his court that the law code known as the *Siete Partidas*, or Seven-Part Code, was composed; he was a great patron of learning and is remembered as Alfonso 'the Wise' or 'the Learned'.)

King James I of Aragon (r.1213–76) captured the Balearic Islands (1229–35) and the kingdom of Valencia (1233–38). Both these campaigns were crusades. James was renowned as *El Conquistador* (the Conqueror). In Portugal, King Sancho II (r.1223–47) reconquered from the Moors a number of cities in Alentejo (south-central Portugal) and the Algarve (the southernmost part of the country). By the close of the 13th century, the kingdom of Granada was the only part of the entire peninsula to remain under Muslim rule.

▼ *Knights embark by sea for the Holy Land on crusade. The illustration is from a book made for Alfonso X of Castile and León, a great patron of court learning who also played his part in the Reconquista.*

THE CONQUEST OF GRANADA
FINAL STAGE OF THE RECONQUISTA

In the 14th and 15th centuries the Muslim kingdom of Granada in southern Spain was the only surviving part of al-Andalus. In theory subordinate to the kingdom of Castile, its ruler a feudal vassal of the King of Castile from the time of King Ferdinand III onwards in the mid-13th century, its days seemed numbered. But remarkably, Granada survived until 1492 when the might of a united Spain, formed by the union of Castile and Aragon, finally brought to an end almost 800 years of Muslim rule in Spain.

MUSLIM HOLY WAR

In Morocco, the Marinids ousted the Almohads, with the aid of Christian mercenaries, in the mid-13th century, taking Fes in 1248 and Marrakech in 1269. The Marinids were fundamentalist Muslims who declared a jihad on the Kingdom of Castile in 1275 and formed an alliance with the Nasrid sultans of Granada; Marinid soldiers helped Granada to protect its borders and even won back some fortified settlements that had fallen to the Christians. The Nasrid sultans ceded the Spanish city of Algeciras to the Marinids.

▼ *Crusading monarchs. This stained glass window celebrates the capture of Malaga by Ferdinand and Isabella's army in 1487.*

SIR JAMES DOUGLAS AND THE BATTLE OF TEBA

King Alfonso XI 'the Implacable' of Castile (r.1312–50) took up the battle against Granada. In 1330 he defeated Sultan Muhammad IV of Granada at the Battle of Teba in Andulasia. In this battle Sir James Douglas, friend of Robert the Bruce, King of Scots, was killed. Douglas had departed from Scotland bearing the Bruce's embalmed heart in order to fulfil his promise to the late king to carry it to the Holy Land; en route he had diverted to Spain to help Alfonso in his struggle against Granada. After the battle, Douglas's body and the Bruce's heart were returned to Scotland, where they were buried.

In the immediate aftermath of his victory at Teba, Alfonso captured the nearby Castle of the Star and installed knights of the military monastic brotherhood of the Order of Santiago as its garrison. Two years later in 1332, in Vittoria, the king founded the chivalric Order of the Sash.

BATTLE OF RIO SALADO

In 1340 Alfonso – together with King Afonso IV 'the Brave' of Portugal (r.1325–57) – defeated a large Marinid army at Rio Salado. The Marinids had amassed a vast army and they crossed the Straits of Gibraltar to mount an invasion with the

▲ *King Ferdinand I of Aragon, the ruler celebrated as 'He of Antequera' after he captured that town from the Muslims as part of the Reconquista, issued this ducat during his brief reign in Aragon, 1412–16.*

aim of establishing their own permanent kingdom in Spain. They captured Gibraltar, defeating a Christian fleet, then moved inland to meet the two Christian kings near Tarifa on the Salado river.

Following a resounding victory over the invaders, Alfonso proceeded to attack Algeciras, which he retook after a two-year siege in 1344. This siege drew Christian volunteers from all over Europe. The defeat of the Marinids at Rio Salado marked the end of the last attempted Muslim invasion of Spain and seemed to clear the way for a final push against Granada. After 1350, however, Alfonso's successors were distracted from the Reconquista by civil war in Castile, and Granada made a number of inroads into Christian territory, taking the city of Jaen, among other strongholds.

In the first part of the 15th century, the Spanish Christian kingdoms moved once more against the Muslim presence. In 1410 the future King Ferdinand I of Aragon (r.1412–16) captured the fortified town of Antequera from Granada while he was regent for his nephew, the infant King John II of Castile. For this feat, he was

▲ *After the end of the Reconquista in 1492, the Jews were expelled from Spain by decree of Ferdinand and Isabella.*

elected to the throne of Aragon and was known as *El de Antequera* (He of Antequera). In 1430 Ferdinand's nephew King John II of Castile (r.1406–54) launched a campaign against Granada that culminated in a victory over the Nasrid sultan Muhammad IX at the Battle of Higuerela, in July 1431.

For almost 50 years thereafter there was no major offensive against Granada. Spanish military brotherhoods, such as the orders of Calatrava and of Santiago, and leading Castilian noblemen conducted a raiding and skirmishing war along the frontier between Castile and Granada, intermittently joined by crusaders seeking glory, riches and crusading privileges.

BIRTH OF SPAIN

In 1469 Ferdinand, heir to the throne of Aragon, married Princess Isabella, heir to the throne of Castile. He became king consort in Castile in 1474 when Isabella became queen following the death of her brother King Henry IV of Castile, and when Ferdinand succeeded his father,

King John II of Aragon (r.1458–79), in 1479, the couple ruled a united kingdom of Aragon and Castile. This marked the birth of the nation of Spain. Within three years they moved against Granada and in a ten-year war, 1482–92, won the final victory of the Reconquista. Ferdinand and Isabella made sure that their army was

equipped with the latest artillery guns and cannon. They promoted the campaign as a religious war – on several occasions Isabella led prayers on or near the field of battle, declaring her burning desire that God's will be performed; soldiers came from several European countries to join the crusade. In Spain, money was raised to cover expenses through the imposition of crusade taxes and the sale of crusade indulgences. The crusaders besieged and captured Ronda in 1485 and took Loja the next year. In 1487 they captured Malaga and in 1489 Baza.

They laid siege to the city of Granada in 1491. After their camp was destroyed by fire, they rebuilt it in stone in the shape of a giant cross, had it painted white and named it Santa Fe (Sacred Faith). At the end of 1491 Sultan Boabdil surrendered the city. Ferdinand and Isabella made a formal entry into Granada on 2 January 1492 and oversaw the reconsecration of the city's main mosque as a church.

▼ *At the gorgeous Alhambra palace in the city of Granada, Sultan Boabdil consults with advisers in 1492, prior to surrendering to the army of Ferdinand and Isabella.*

THE ALBIGENSIAN CRUSADE
WAR ON HERESY

In 1208 a papal legate named Pierre of Castelnau was murdered in the Languedoc region of southern France and Pope Innocent III (ruled 1198–1216) declared a crusade against the Cathars of that region, who were viewed as heretics by the Catholic Church. The Cathars were subsequently called the Albigensians (from the town of Albi that was inaccurately identified as their headquarters).

The Albigensian crusade lasted 20 years, from 1209 to 1229, and although it began as a religious war aimed at curbing what the Church hierarchy saw as a popular and dangerous heresy, it became little more than an exercise in territorial expansion by northern French barons. The

▲ *The seal of Raymond VI of Toulouse. It was his vassal who murdered Pierre of Castelnau and provoked Pope Innocent to declare his crusade against the Cathars.*

▼ *St Dominic worked for years to convince the Cathars that their beliefs were heretical. After the celebrated trial by fire, in which Cathar books burned while orthodox Catholic volumes were spared, he gave one of the orthodox books to the Cathars.*

religious victory over the Cathars when it came was achieved not in battle but through the efforts of the Dominican Inquisition (a tribunal to investigate heresy), established in 1233. Military action against the Cathars continued inter-

mittently until 1255. The Cathars were driven from France into Italy, where they died out and were heard of no more after the end of the 14th century.

CATHAR BELIEFS AND BACKGROUND

The Cathars took their name from the Greek word *katharos*, meaning 'pure'. They were dualists, believing in two gods – an ultimate embodiment of goodness, and a lesser and evil creator god who had made the material world. They believed the material world therefore to be evil: the human soul was naturally good and trapped in this evil creation; people should seek salvation through extreme asceticism. Cathars avoided meat and animal products, were sexually chaste, lived in poverty and were pacifists.

Cathars divided themselves into two groups: 'the perfect' and 'the believers'. The perfect passed through an initiation ceremony called the *consolamentum* and

lived lives of extreme asceticism, devoting their energy to contemplation. The believers were not required to attain the very high standards of asceticism and religious devotion attained by the perfect.

ROOTS IN GNOSTICISM

Cathar beliefs may have derived from ancient Gnosticism, a dualist faith system popular in the Mediterranean and Middle East from the last centuries BC onward, but suppressed in the Christian Roman Empire from the 4th century AD. Like Cathars, Gnostics believed in dual divinities. The highest god was good and the lesser one evil; the evil one had created the material world. Humans were divine souls trapped in the material world, from which they could only escape through *gnosis* or knowledge held by the elite. The Cathars did not place strong emphasis on spiritual knowledge, but they did have an initiation ceremony, and an initiated elite.

BOGOMILS AND PAULICIANS

The Cathars certainly had links with the Gnostic-influenced Christian groups of the Bogomils and the Paulicians. The Bogomils had emerged in the 10th century in Bulgaria and spread from there into the Byzantine Empire, as well as into Italy and France: they were dualists, who rejected the doctrine of Christ's divine birth and the veneration of the Virgin Mary and declared that reverence for the cross and for saintly relics was no more than idolatry.

The Paulicians had their origins earlier, in the 7th–9th centuries, in Armenia: they rejected the Old Testament, veneration of the Virgin Mary, worship of the Cross and the sacraments of Baptism and Communion. The Cathars for their part denied the divinity of Christ and declared him to have been an angel come to earth; they said that his apparent sufferings and death as a human being were an illusion. Cathar teaching also rejected the doctrines of purgatory and hell and that of the resurrection of the body, arguing in favour of reincarnation.

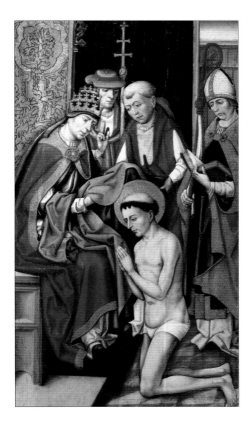

▲ *Pope Innocent III sent out wandering preachers to bring heretics back to the true faith. He gave St Dominic and St Francis (shown here) his blessing to do this work.*

The Cathars were first established in Flanders, northern Italy and western Germany in 1000–50. They expanded in 1140–70, particularly under the influence of a resurgent Bogomil Church that sent missionaries throughout Europe; historians also believe that soldiers and pilgrims on the First Crusade picked up dualist ideas and brought them back to Europe in the early 12th century. In the 1140s the Cathars established themselves as a church: their first bishop in *c.*1149 was in northern France, but soon afterward he was joined by counterparts in Lombardy and in Albi. By 1200 they had five bishops in France and six in Italy.

SERIOUS THREAT

Remarkably, in the Languedoc Catharism became a popular religion – unlike many sects, attracting a wide following among the nobility, educated townspeople and the peasantry. Cathars attacked the wealth

and corruption of the Church, while rejecting the authority of Catholic priests and of the pope; they posed a threat to the very structure of society, for they rejected the taking of oaths that was one of the central features of the feudal system. Moreover, the fact that they had many followers among both nobility and peasantry served to undo the natural, God-given social hierarchy that orthodox believers saw in the feudal system.

Pope Innocent III initially tried to bring the Cathars back to orthodoxy by peaceful means, sending preachers – including Dominic Guzman (later St Dominic), founder of the Dominican Order – to attempt to convert the heretics. The preachers had little success. Innocent then found that local nobles and even bishops were protecting the Cathars. In 1204 he suspended the bishops and replaced them with papal legates, and he demanded that Philip II of France (r.1180–1223) force the nobles to return to Catholicism. Philip refused to take action. Innocent demanded that the powerful local count, Raymond VI of Toulouse, take action but he, too, refused and was excommunicated.

In January 1208 Raymond held a meeting with the papal legate, Pierre of Castelnau, which ended angrily. The following day Pierre of Castelnau was murdered by one of Raymond's vassals. Pope Innocent III declared war, issuing a call to a crusade against the Cathars.

Innocent offered a full crusade indulgence to all who responded to his call to take up arms against the Cathars. He also declared that they would have the right to seize the land of the heretics, which attracted a number of northern French barons to the cause. It should be noted that the indulgence offered to the anti-Cathar crusaders was remarkably generous – the annulment of sins was being offered for a mere 40 days campaigning (the normal period of feudal military service) and for a war fought in nearby southern France rather than for a potentially very hazardous journey over land and sea to the Holy Land.

MASSACRE OF THE CATHARS
TWENTY YEARS OF BRUTAL WAR, 1209–1229

The crusade armies raised against the Cathars by Pope Innocent III won a series of brutal victories in 1209–15, in which local people – both Cathars and Catholics – were slaughtered in their thousands. During the next ten years, many of these bloody victories were overturned by rebels, but in 1226 King Louis VIII of France (r.1223–26) entered the fray on the side of the Church and following his death in November that year, his son Louis IX (r.1226–70) took up the fight. The Languedoc region was conquered by 1229 and peace was finally agreed in the Treaty of Paris that year.

COUNT RAYMOND RECANTS

In 1209 a crusade army of around 10,000 massed in Lyon and marched south under the leadership of papal legate Arnaul Amalric, Abbot of Cîteaux. Suddenly persuaded of the error of his ways, Raymond VI of Toulouse agreed at last to move against the Cathars and was reconciled to the Church in a ceremony before carvings of the Passion of Christ on the west front

▼ *At the Battle of Muret on 12 September 1213, Simon of Montfort's small crusader force roundly defeated the much larger army of Peter II of Aragon and Raymond of Toulouse. Peter was killed in action.*

of the Benedictine abbey church of Saint-Gilles. The crusaders then marched towards Montpellier; Raymond-Roger Trencavel, viscount of Béziers and Albi and a vassal of Raymond VI of Toulouse, attempted to make peace with them but was refused an audience. He fled back to Carcassonne to arrange its defence.

THE SLAUGHTER AT BÉZIERS

The crusade army marched to Béziers, where it arrived on 21 July 1209. The soldiers demanded the surrender of the Cathars and the submission of any local Catholics; both groups refused. But the crusaders gained access to the town when an attempted sortie by the defenders went wrong and they burned Béziers to the ground and savagely killed every man, woman and child.

According to one account, soldiers asked the Abbot of Cîteaux how they would tell Cathars from Catholics and the abbot replied: 'Kill them all. God will recognize his own.' Afterwards the Abbot wrote gleefully to the Pope: 'Our soldiers spared neither rank, nor sex, nor elderly. About 20,000 people lost their lives … the entire city was put to the sword. Thus did God's vengeance vent its wondrous rage.'

CATHARS EVICTED FROM CARCASSONNE

Many settlements were terrified into submission and surrendered to the army. The crusaders marched on Carcassonne and took it after a two-week siege on 15 August 1209. The Cathars were forcibly evicted, having been stripped naked to humiliate them. At this point, French nobleman Simon of Montfort took charge of the crusade army and was granted territory that included the Cathar strongholds of Carcassonne, Albi and Béziers. (Simon of Montfort, a veteran of the Fourth Crusade, was the father of Simon of Montfort, 6th Earl of Leicester and main

▲ *Fighting during the siege of Carcassonne. In the rear the Cathars emerge from the city to take on the besieging crusaders.*

leader of baronial opposition to King Henry III of England; the 6th Earl was the effective ruler of England in 1263–64 and is remembered as a pioneer of parliamentary democracy.)

Town after town surrendered or was conquered by the crusader army over the following months. In June–July 1210 the city of Minerve put up a brave resistance but finally surrendered on 22 July; many Cathars accepted Catholicism, but fully 140 remained defiant and were burned at the stake. In 1211 Raymond of Toulouse was again excommunicated after he fell out with Simon of Montfort. In May hundreds of Cathars were burned at the stake and Aimery of Montréal was hanged after his castle fell to Montfort.

The crusaders besieged Raymond in Toulouse, but the siege failed and the army withdrew. Raymond then led a successful rebellion, capturing Castelnaudary from Simon of Montfort and 'freeing' more than 30 towns for the Cathar cause.

THE BATTLE OF MURET

In 1212, however, much of Toulouse was captured. In 1213 King Peter II of Aragon (r.1196–1213), famous victor over the Moors at the battle of Las Navas de Tolosa, led an army in support of Raymond, who was his brother-in-law. With Raymond, he besieged Montfort in Muret, but was defeated and killed in the ensuing battle. The Aragonese army broke and fled on seeing their king slain.

In 1214, Raymond was forced to flee to England and his lands were given by the pope to Philip II, who became involved in the war. In 1214–16 Montfort captured the remaining Cathar strongholds and also ceded his lands to Philip II.

CATHAR RESURGENCE

In 1216 the tide began to turn. In that year, Pope Innocent III died and was replaced by Honorius III (r.1216–27), who was not so strongly committed to waging war on the Cathars. Raymond returned from exile and captured first Beaucaire and then, in 1217, Toulouse. Montfort besieged him there and was killed in fighting outside the city on 25 June 1218, his head crushed by a stone hurled from a mangonel. The Cathar side made a number of gains, including

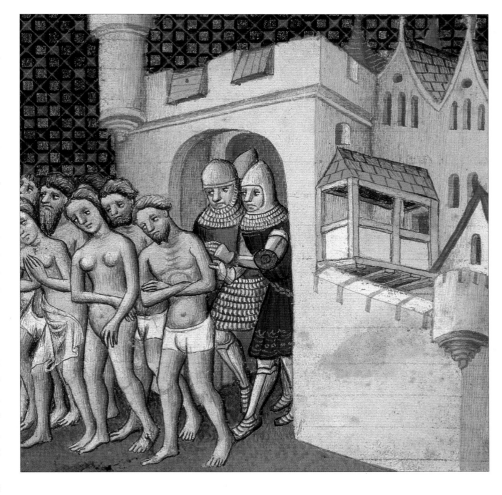

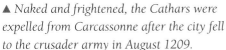

▼ *The Cathar stronghold of Carcassonne had grown from a Roman fortification, and parts of its northern walls date from when France was under Roman rule.*

Castelnaudary, Montreal and Fanjeaux and, in 1224, Carcassonne. Raymond VI of Toulouse had died in 1222 , and been succeeded by his son, another Raymond; and Philip II had died, in 1223, and been succeeded by King Louis VIII. Amaury of Montfort, son of Simon, offered his claim to territory in the Languedoc to the new French king, who took up the challenge.

▲ *Naked and frightened, the Cathars were expelled from Carcassonne after the city fell to the crusader army in August 1209.*

Louis led a new crusade army into the region in June 1226. Many castles and towns surrendered without a fight but it took a three-month siege to capture Avignon. That same autumn, Louis VIII died and was succeeded by his son, Louis IX, at the age of just 12. Louis VIII's widow, Blanche of Castile, acted as regent and ordered the continuation of the crusade under the command of Humbert of Beaujeu. The crusaders crushed Cathar resistance, taking Labécède in 1227 and Toulouse in 1228.

A peace treaty was finally agreed in 1229 under which Count Raymond was recognized as ruler of Toulouse, but was forced to agree to hand his castles over into royal control, to dismantle the defences of Toulouse and to attempt to suppress the Cathars.

THE CATHAR INQUISITION
THE FAITHFUL BESIEGED – WITH SECRET TREASURE?

In 1233 Pope Gregory IX (ruled 1227–41) established a papal Inquisition (or investigative tribunal) staffed by Dominican friars charged with stamping out the Cathars. Many of the heretics were burned at the stake, while others fled the Inquisition to northern Italy. A few Cathar communities survived in isolated fortresses in the Pyrenees but these were gradually captured by the royalist forces. The Castle of Montségur was taken in March 1244 after a nine-month siege, while the small fort of Quéribus, probably the last surviving Cathar stronghold, was taken in August 1255.

The Dominican Inquisition was given substantial powers to stamp out heresy by burning Cathars where they were found and even in some cases digging up the bodies of former heretics to burn them. In a letter of 1233, the pope denounced the preachers of the Cathar faith as 'evil min-

▼ *An enthroned Pope Gregory IX hears the report of a Dominican inquisitor.*

▲ *The mountaintop Castle of Quéribus may have been the Cathars' last refuge. It was rebuilt by the French as one of five castles that guarded the French border with Spain.*

isters of Satan … they appear to be pious but they entirely deny all virtue. Their sermons are smoother than the oil of crushed olives; but they are as dangerous as javelins and their words have a sting in the tail like that of a scorpion.' He urged the Dominican priors to 'root out … the wickedness of heresy', 'to work assiduously against all who receive, help or defend any who are excommunicated'; he encouraged them to 'lay sentences of interdict' on the lands of those behaved in this way. But he also encouraged them to give absolution to those that 'wish to come back to the unity of the church'. He made a promise that all who came to listen to the sermons of the friars would be granted freedom from 20 days' penance.

CATHAR REVOLTS

The Cathars continued to resist. They drove the friars of the Inquisition out of Narbonne, Toulouse and Albi in 1235. Another Raymond, son of Roger Trencavel, led a revolt in 1240 and attempted to capture Carcassonne. But he was driven off and then besieged by the forces of King Louis IX in the Castle of Montréal. Raymond escaped and fled into exile in Aragon. (Later he surrendered to Louis, and accompanied the king on the Seventh Crusade.)

In 1242 Count Raymond VIII of Toulouse tried to mount a revolt in alliance with the English, but the campaign faltered, the English were defeated by Louis IX at Taillebourg and the rebellion came to nothing. Count Raymond surrendered to Louis and asked for his excommunication to be lifted. Many Cathars took refuge in mountain strongholds such as Montségur. The Council of Béziers determined in the spring of 1243 to attack the castle there as an attempt to wipe out Catharism once and for all.

SIEGE OF MONTSÉGUR

The Castle of Montségur was perched atop a rock at an altitude of 3,900ft (1,200m) in the Languedoc near the Pyrenees Mountains. It was built on the ruins of an earlier fortress by Raymond of Pereille in c.1210. According to some accounts, it was the headquarters of the Cathars in the Languedoc region.

▲ *Roman Catholic monks rejoice at the burning of the Cathars at Montségur.*

From May 1243 to March 1244 it was besieged by a royalist army of around 10,000 commanded by Hugh of Arcis, Louis IX's Seneschal of Carcassonne. On 1 March 1244 the defenders, offered terms of surrender, asked for a two-week truce to consider them; in return they provided hostages whose lives would be forfeit if the defenders tried to flee. On March 14, the defenders reportedly celebrated a festival coinciding with the spring equinox. On the next day the truce expired, and around 220 Cathars, all members of their initiated elite group 'the perfect', were taken down the mountainside and burned as heretics in a large stockade at the foot of the hill. In the two-week period, an additional 25 of the Cathars had joined the ranks of 'the perfect' and were therefore put to death.

ESCAPE WITH TREASURE?

In the final days of the siege, it is said that four of the castle defenders slipped unnoticed though the siege lines carrying some unidentified treasure. This treasure may have been esoteric writings, Cathar riches or, as some claim, the Holy Grail.

One tradition claims that the Knights Templar when building on Temple Mount in Jerusalem discovered extraordinary treasure that they then passed to the Cathars, and that these treasures were among those smuggled out of Montségur. Some writers claim that the castle may have been the actual Holy Grail castle celebrated in chivalric romances and poems such as *Parzival* by Wolfram von Eschenbach (written only decades earlier, in 1200–10) – where the Grail castle is called Monsalvat, strikingly similar to Montségur. (The Castle of Montségur that survives today is not the one that was occupied by the Cathars, for that fortress was entirely destroyed by the royalist army in 1244. The building seen today was built over the ensuing centuries and has many characteristics typical of the 1600s.)

The few surviving Cathars gathered in another hilltop stronghold at Quéribus. When a French army was despatched to deal with them in 1255 they fled the castle without a fight and left the country, dispersing to take refuge either in Aragon or in northern Italy.

LINKS TO TEMPLARS?

One reason that the Knights Templar came under such fierce attack in the early 14th century was that they were accused of fraternizing with and protecting heretics. The sixth Templar Grand Master, Bertrand of Blanchefort (Grand Master 1156–69) was reputedly from a Cathar family and from his time the Templars accepted Cathars into the order. The Templars accepted many heretics into their ranks because recruitment was always difficult, but they had a significant number of Cathar members from France. During the Albigensian Crusade the Templars gave refuge to Cathars fleeing the crusaders – and allowed them to bury their dead in their Templar graveyards.

▼ *Was the Cathar fortress at Montségur in south-western France the original Grail castle? The current castle was erected on the ruins of the Cathar one in the 1600s.*

THE BALTIC CRUSADES

HOLY WAR AGAINST NORTHERN PAGANS

The Baltic Crusades were military campaigns against the pagan peoples on the southern and eastern shores of the Baltic Sea. They were cast as wars of religion but were often fought to gain territory for local bishops and feudal lords. The Baltic Crusades are often said to have started in the 1190s when popes Celestine III and Innocent III called what became a standing crusade. Its purpose was to support the Catholic Church in the region of Livonia (now Estonia, Lithuania and Latvia), but as early as 1147 crusading privileges had been officially granted to Saxon, Danish and Polish Christians fighting against the pagan Wends of the Baltic.

THE WENDISH CRUSADE

In 1147 when Bernard of Clairvaux was preaching the Second Crusade to the Holy Land on behalf of Pope Eugenius III, he was told by the north German Saxons that they were not willing to travel to the Holy Land but wanted to conduct a holy war against the pagan Wends in the Baltic. Eugenius sent out the *Divina dispensatione*

▲ *The Baltic Crusades had begun as much as 50 years before Pope Celestine III called a crusade in Livonia following the failure of a Church mission to the region.*

bull, on 13 April 1147, guaranteeing those fighting on this Baltic crusade the same benefits as those who took the cross to fight in the Holy Land. Bernard himself wrote of the crusaders' attack on the Wends: 'We expressly forbid that for any cause they should agree peace with these people until either their false religion or their nation has been destroyed.'

Papal legate Anselm of Havelberg was put in command of an army that included Danes and Poles as well as Saxons. Some of these crusaders were genuinely fighting in order to convert the pagans, but many bishops and lords were primarily seeking to increase their landholding in the region.

◀ *The Wends of the Baltic region were descendants of Slavic tribes who settled in eastern Germany in the 5th century AD. King Wandalus was a mythical ancestor, and was supposedly originally a Trojan.*

The campaign followed the annexation by Count Adolph of Holstein of Wendish lands, which he had parcelled out among Christian immigrants from western Germany. Wendish leader Niklot led an invasion of Wagria (now eastern Holstein in northern Germany) and Adolph fought back with part of the crusader army. This part of the campaign was swiftly over, and ended in a peace treaty, but other crusaders attacked Dobin and Demmin. At Dobin, the members of the Wendish garrison were baptized following a siege. The crusade army marching on Demmin sacked a castle and pagan temple at Malchow, but their siege of Demmin was unsuccessful and so they marched on into

Pomerania on the Baltic coast where, reaching the Christian city of Stettin (now in Poland), they were greeted by Bishop Albert of Pomerania and Prince Ratorbor I of Pomerania and then disbanded.

The crusade achieved a few conversions, but many of these Christianized Wends reverted to their own religion after the crusaders left. It had the effect of strengthening Christian landholdings in the region and of weakening the resistance of the local people to future campaigns.

THE CRUSADE IN LIVONIA

Before Celestine and Innocent unleashed the power of the crusading machine on Livonia in the 1190s, the Church had made peaceful efforts to convert the local populace. In the 11th century Adalbert, Archbishop of Bremen in 1045–72, had sent missionaries into the region, but with little effect. In 1180 an Augustinian monk called Meinhard led missionary work at Uxhull (modern Ikskile) on the River Dvina (now called the Daugava) and established himself as bishop.

▼ *Prince Niklot, who fought against the crusade army in 1147, had renounced Christianity and reverted to paganism. He is an ancestor of the dukes of Mecklenburg, and is honoured with this statue in their castle at Schwerin, north-eastern Germany.*

▲ *The Livonian Brothers of the Sword fought in Finland in 1232 on the orders of Pope Gregory IX. After they merged with the Teutonic Knights in 1236, they still had their own Master. He was subject to the Grand Master of the Teutonic Knights.*

After Meinhard's successor, Berthold, reported that the mission to Livonia was close to failure, Pope Celestine III called a crusade in the area. A Saxon crusading army led by Berthold won a battle against the Livonians in 1198, but Berthold was killed. Subsequently the crusaders went home and the missionary monks had to abandon their work after the Livonians issued death threats against them.

In 1199 the Archbishop Hartwig of Bremen appointed his nephew Albert of Buxhoeveden as Bishop of Livonia, with instructions to conquer the region and impose Christianity on its people. Albert embarked on a tour to preach a crusade in Livonia, and Pope Innocent III issued a papal bull guaranteeing those who fought in Livonia the same crusading privileges as knights and men-at-arms fighting in the Holy Land. At the bishop's request, Innocent also dedicated the Baltic region to the Virgin Mary, in order to encourage recruits to the cause, and the area is still sometimes known as 'Mary's Land'.

In 1200 Albert landed at the mouth of the River Dvina with a crusade army of around 1,500 men aboard a fleet of 23 vessels. In the next year he abandoned his mission station at Uxhull and founded the trading settlement of Riga at the mouth of the river. Previous efforts at conquest had foundered when temporary crusading armies disbanded, so in 1202 he founded the military order of the Livonian Brothers of the Sword to ensure a continuous military presence. (Albert founded the Cathedral of Riga in 1215; he was later named a Prince of the Holy Roman Empire, with Livonia as his fief, and was known as a 'Prince-Bishop'.) The Livonian Brothers of the Sword suffered a heavy defeat at the hands of a Livonian army in 1236 and the order's few survivors joined the Teutonic Knights.

For more than 25 years, until his death in 1229, Albert was engaged in the conquest of Livonia. He converted some of the locals – for example the Livs accepted Christianity when Bishop Albert guaranteed them military protection against incursion by rival Lithuanians and Estonian tribes; he also achieved the conversion of some Latvians. Otherwise he achieved his goals by military means. By c.1230 the conquest and conversion of Livonia was complete.

▼ *The seal of the Livonian Brothers of the Sword. They were called* Fratres militiae Christi Livoniae *in Latin.*

IN PRUSSIA AND LITHUANIA

EUROPEAN CRUSADES OF THE TEUTONIC KNIGHTS

Over a period of 50 years of brutal campaigning from *c*.1230 onwards, the military brotherhood of the Teutonic Knights imposed Christianity on the pagan peoples of Prussia. The Teutonic Knights, who had been founded in the Holy Land but were seeking to establish themselves in central Europe, entered Prussia under an agreement that allowed them to keep their initial landholding and all that they conquered. As a result they built up a substantial territory, which they ruled as a sovereign monastic state, answerable only to the Holy Roman Emperor and the papacy. In the 14th century, having conquered Prussia, they led a series of campaigns against Lithuania. These campaigns attracted knights from France and England to test their chivalric attributes in battle.

In 1209 Christian, a Cistercian monk from the monastery of Oliva (modern Oliwa, part of Gdasnk in northern Poland)

▼ *Grand Master of the Teutonic Knights. The brotherhood needed shrewd leadership as it attempted to find a new role and a new base in Europe in the 1200s.*

HENRY BOLINGBROKE'S CRUSADE

In 1390, after taking part in the celebrated Jousts of St Ingelvert near Calais, Henry intended to lead a small army of around 120 men on a crusade against Muslims in Tunisia, but because he was not granted safe conduct through France he joined the Teutonic Knights on a *reysen* against the Lithuanians. With 32 knights and squires he sailed to Danzig (now northern Poland), arriving on 10 August and joining the knights' march up the River Niemen. He took part in the siege of Vilnius from 4 September and after its failure returned to the Teutonic Knights' headquarters at Marienburg (now Malbork in Poland), where he remained for the winter, enjoying the feasting, hunting and other

▲ *Henry Bolingbroke (right) accompanies King Richard II as he enters London.*

chivalric entertainments. He departed at the end of March 1391. We know from royal records that the expedition cost him no less than £4,360.

was appointed by Pope Innocent III to lead missions in Prussia. He was named the first Bishop of Prussia in 1212. The mission came under repeated attacks from pagan Prussians and in 1217 Pope Honorius III (r.1216–27) called a crusade in the region.

The Prussians launched another major attack in 1218, in the course of which they sacked no fewer than 300 churches and cathedrals. A crusade army gathered in Masovia (now eastern Poland) from 1219 onwards and engaged the enemy without fighting a major campaign; the bishopric of Prussia was given a number of territories by Christian lords, meanwhile, in the area of Chelmno Land (now central Poland). The Prussians launched another devastating attack on Chelmno Land and Masovia in 1223.

Bishop Christian and Duke Konrad I of Masovia decided to establish an intimidating and permanent military presence to deter further Prussian raids. In 1225–28, on the border between Masovia

and Prussia (modern Dobrzyn Land in Poland), Christian established the Order of Dobrzyn, also known as the *Fratres Milites Christi de Prussia* or 'the Prussian Cavaliers of Christ Jesus'. At around the same time, Konrad invited the Teutonic Knights to help defend his borders against the Prussian raiders.

TEUTONIC KNIGHTS

The Teutonic Knights had been founded in 1192 as a monastic brotherhood in charge of a German hospital in Acre and then become a military brotherhood in Outremer in 1198. At the start of the 13th century they had established a presence in eastern Europe, entering the service of King Andrew II of Hungary in 1211, but after a disagreement Andrew had expelled the brothers from the territory he had granted them in Burzenland, Transylvania.

When Duke Konrad invited the Teutonic Knights to Masovia, the brotherhood was still heavily committed in Outremer: the first contingent of Teutonic

Knights despatched to Masovia numbered just seven knights and around 100 squires and sergeants. From an initial base at Vogelsang, south of the River Vistula, they concentrated on establishing timber fortresses along the line of the river. Reinforcements, numbering around 20 knights and 200 sergeants, arrived at Vogelsang in c.1230. They campaigned only when German and Polish crusaders arrived to swell their numbers. By 1232 the Knights and crusaders had defeated the Prussians in Chelmno Land.

Pope Gregory IX (ruled 1227–41) called for crusaders to back the Teutonic Knights in their struggle and a crusade army of 10,000 men gathered in the summer of 1233. In 1233–34 they won significant territorial gains, consolidated with fortresses at Marienwerder (now Kwidzyn in northern Poland) and Rehden (modern Radzyn Chelminski).

On these foundations the Teutonic Knights built a great edifice. In the course of many long and bloody campaigns over no less than 50 years they gradually defeated the Prussians. There were several Prussian uprisings: in 1242, most seriously in 1260–74, and again in 1286 and in 1295, but by the end of the 13th century the Knights had imposed their authority completely on Prussia.

ASSIMILATING OTHER ORDERS

The Order of Dobrzyn did not have a long or glorious existence. The initial membership was just 15 knights, and at its largest the order had only 35 knights. In c.1235 most of the knights joined the Teutonic Order. In the following year, 1236, the Livonian Brothers of the Sword, the brotherhood established by Albert of Buxhoeveden in 1202, was comprehensively defeated by an army of pagan Samogitians at the Battle of Saule and was also assimilated by the Teutonic Knights.

MONASTIC STATE

The Teutonic Knights had moved to Prussia on the understanding that they would be given a base in Chelmno Land

as a permanent territory of their own and would be allowed to keep any land they conquered. This agreement was not recognized by Duke Konrad or Bishop Christian, but was guaranteed by Holy Roman Emperor Frederick II in the 'Golden Bull of Rimini' of 1226 and by Pope Gregory IX in the 'Golden Bull of Rieti' of 1234. The Knights governed the territory they carved out for themselves in Prussia as a 'monastic state'. They were subject only to the Holy Roman Emperor and the papacy.

14TH-CENTURY CRUSADES

Throughout the 14th century the Teutonic Knights led a series of crusading campaigns against the pagan Lithuanians. Following the fall of Acre in 1291 to the Mamluks, the great knights of Europe had no outlet in the Holy Land for their crusading ambitions and they saw the Teutonic Knights' annual manoeuvres in Lithuania as an opportunity to prove their martial prowess, have a taste of crusading glory – and perhaps relive some of the storied exploits of past knights of the cross.

The Teutonic Knights ran their campaigns like adventure holidays, laying on feasts, courtly hunting expeditions and prizes. Knights came from all over Europe – especially from England and France – to take part; in Chaucer's *The Canterbury Tales* his Knight takes part in one of the Teutonic adventures. The campaigns were called *reysen* (voyages): those who took

▲ *The Teutonic Knights built a vast castle as their new headquarters at Marienburg (Mary's Castle) in Prussia in 1309.*

part had to cross a 100 mile (160km) wide area of swampland and forest, which they called 'the wilderness' before engaging the enemy.

It was in the interests of all involved in the *reysen* to maintain the pretence that these annual chivalric adventures were genuine crusades, fought to bring the Christian faith to an obdurately pagan people. The campaigns became so popular that they continued even after the Lithuanians were converted to Christianity in 1386. For all that fantasy played its part, the military element, it must be stressed, was real enough – the fighting when it came was as brutal as in any war, and prisoners taken were treated with contempt since they were pagan.

Among the many great names connected to the *reysen* were French knight Jean Le Meingre, Marshal of France and known as 'Boucicaut', who fought on three campaigns in Lithuania as a young man, and King Henry IV of England, who in his youth (while Henry Bolingbroke, Earl of Derby) took part in a campaign of 1390 that culminated in the siege of the Lithuanian capital, Vilnius. He subsequently looked back with great pleasure on the experience; he was still talking of the Teutonic Knights with warmth and affection some 17 years later, in 1407.

CRUSADES AGAINST THE HUSSITES

BOHEMIA UNDER ATTACK

Five crusades were launched against the Hussites in Bohemia in 1420–32. Followers of a university lecturer and preacher, Jan Hus, who had been burned at the stake for heresy in 1415, the Hussites were inspired by the beginnings of Czech nationalist feeling and challenged the rule of King Sigismund of Hungary in their homeland. None of the crusades achieved its goal and Sigismund was forced to agree a compromise in 1436.

HUS

Jan Hus was Dean of the philosophical faculty at Prague University from 1401 and a supporter of reform of the Roman Catholic Church in Bohemia. He established himself as a popular preacher through his sermons in Czech (rather than Latin) at the Bethlehem Chapel in Prague and was a leader of a national reform movement. He was excommunicated by Pope Alexander V (ruled 1409–10) in 1409 after refusing to accept a papal ban on preaching in private chapels. He was called to the Council of Constance in 1415 and promised safe conduct, but while he was there he was condemned as a heretic and burned at the stake.

His execution sparked protests in Bohemia, where Bohemian knights and nobility made a formal protest, the *protestatio Bohemorum*, and offered support and protection to people persecuted for their religious faith. When King Wenceslaus IV of Bohemia died in 1419, his half-brother King Sigismund of Hungary (later Holy Roman Emperor, 1433–37) claimed the throne. The Bohemian nobles rejected his claim, however, and installed their own government, starting the 'Hussite Revolt', which had the support of reforming clergy and townspeople as well as the nobility.

THE FIRST CRUSADE (1420)

In a bull of 17 March 1420 Pope Martin V (ruled 1417–31) called a crusade against the Hussites, to be led by Sigismund with the support of German princes. Sigismund marched an army swelled by crusaders from all over Europe towards Prague, and besieged the Hussites there at the end of

◄ *Hus defends his beliefs at the Council of Constance. His execution fanned discontent in Bohemia and led to the Hussite Revolt.*

June, but without success. He had himself crowned king of Bohemia in the fortress of Hradcany Castle, but was defeated by the Hussites on 1 November near Pankrac. The Hussites gained control of most of Bohemia after Sigismund withdrew.

HUSSITE DEMANDS AND DIVISIONS

Following the siege of Prague in 1420, Hus's successor at the Bethlehem Chapel, Jakoubek of Stribo, drew up the Four Articles of Prague, which helped establish common ground for the Hussite movement. They called for: freedom in preaching; support for the doctrine of Ultraquism, which required that the faithful should be given both bread and wine in the communion service; the clergy to adopt a lifestyle of poverty; and mortal sins to be prohibited and punished.

▼ *Jan Zizka, inspirational Hussite leader and a great general, commands the rebels in an attack on a small town in Bohemia.*

▶ *Sigismund I of Hungary leads an army against the rebels during the Second Anti-Hussite Crusade, early in 1421. The venture ended in a heavy defeat for the crusaders at the Battle of Nemecky Brod.*

Almost from the beginning, however, the Hussites were split into two camps. Moderate Hussites were called 'Utraquists' from their support for the doctrine of Ultraquism; but there was a more radical wing, often known as 'Taborites' after the city of Tabor. Led by Jan Zizka, the Taborites believed the Millennium or New Age of Christ was at hand and called for a return to innocence and the establishment of a communist-style society in which servants and masters would be no more.

THE SECOND ANTI-HUSSITE CRUSADE (1421)

A German army arrived in Bohemia in August 1421 and besieged Zatec, but after a failed attempt to take the town retreated to avoid an approaching Hussite army. After Sigismund joined the crusaders at the end of the year, he seized the town of Kutna Hora, but on 6 January 1422 was utterly defeated by a Hussite army led by Jan Zizka at the Battle of Nemecky Brod.

THE THIRD CRUSADE FAILS

In 1422–23 there was civil war between the rival Hussite groups in Bohemia: on 27 April 1423 a Taborite army led by Jan Zizka defeated the Utraquist forces at the Battle of Horic. A third crusade had been called, meanwhile, and an army gathered, but it came to nothing amid dissension, and the force dispersed without even attempting to invade Bohemia.

Zizka won further victories over the Utraquists in 1423–24, but died of the plague on 11 October 1424 as he was preparing an invasion of Moravia. Chronicle accounts report that his last wish was for his skin to be made into drums, so that he could continue to lead his men into battle. His soldiers were so distraught at his passing that from that time they called themselves 'the Orphans'.

THE FOURTH AND FIFTH CRUSADES (1427 AND 1431)

Under the leadership of Zizka's successor, Prokop the Great, the Hussite army conducted a series of military raids – which they called 'beautiful rides' – into neighbouring territories. Two further crusades in 1427 and 1431 came to nothing. On the first occasion a crusader army under Frederick, Margarve of Brandenburg, and Cardinal Henry Beaufort, Archbishop-elect of Trier, was defeated at Tachov. In this battle, the crusaders attempted to use the Hussite tactics of the Wagenburg, but were defeated. On the second crusade, a large crusader force entered Bohemia but fled before a Hussite army under Prokop.

PEACE AT LAST

Internal Hussite conflicts were brought to an end at the Battle of Lipany (or Cesky Brod) on 30 May 1434 when the Taborite army under Prokop the Great was roundly defeated by an alliance of Utraquist nobles and Catholics (the 'Bohemian League'). Finally, with more moderate Hussites having won the day, a peace was agreed with Sigismund on 5 July 1436.

HUSSITE BATTLE TACTICS

A key to the Hussite success in battle was the use of *wagenburg* (war wagon) tactics. Horse-drawn war wagons were set in a defensive circle, and a ditch dug around the formation. Each wagon had a crew of 22 foot soldiers and bowmen: eight crossbowmen, two gunners, eight men armed with pikes and flails, two drivers and two shield carriers. In the first phase they used the wagons as a defensive barrier, from behind which they fired their small cannon and handguns; usually the enemy knights were drawn into an attack and the wagenburgers were able to cause carnage among them. The second stage was to burst out from behind the wagons and attack the enemy on the flanks with pikes while the gunners kept up the barrage of fire from behind the wagons.

▶ *Military historians see the* wagenburg *as the forerunner of the tank.*

THE END OF THE CRUSADES

ITALIAN CRUSADES IN THE PAPAL INTEREST

In the 12th–14th centuries a series of crusades were called against Christian princes and noblemen who had been declared enemies of the Catholic Church in Italy. Many of these enterprises were in fact thinly disguised attempts to enforce the interests of the papacy.

In the 12th century the popes established themselves as secular rulers of a strip of territory across the middle of what is now Italy. As early as the 1120s, crusading indulgences were offered to those fighting the opponents of the papacy.

In the 12th and 13th centuries, Italy was divided between the Guelphs (those who supported the papacy) and the Ghibellines (who supported the rule in Italy of the Holy Roman Emperors). The names of the Guelphs and Ghibellines probably derived from rallying cries used at the Battle of Weinsberg (1140) between the house of Hohenstaufen, who called the name of a castle, 'Waiblingen!' (later Ghibelline) and the rival house of Welf, who shouted 'Welf!' (later Guelph), which had the support of the papacy.

▼ *The people of Sicily rise up against Charles I and his French followers in 1282.*

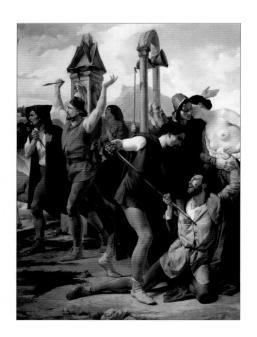

MARKWARD OF ANWEILER

At the close of the 12th century Pope Innocent III (ruled 1198–1216) called a crusade against Markward of Anweiler. His service to the emperors in Italy brought him into territorial conflict with the papacy and he was excommunicated by both Celestine III and Innocent III.

Following Emperor Henry VI's death Markward entered the service of the emperor's brother, Philip of Swabia, by whom he was granted the lordship of Palermo in Sicily. In 1199 Innocent declared a crusade against Markward, claiming he was working in alliance with Muslims resident in Sicily to undermine preparations for the Fourth Crusade. Knights who fought Markward were to receive the same indulgences as those who travelled to the Holy Land on crusade.

Although Innocent excommunicated Markward, and suggested that he was in league with Muslims, Innocent did not accuse Markward of being a heretic, so the cause of the war remained transparently political rather than religious; many historians identify it as the first purely political crusade, even though militarily speaking it did not come to anything.

CRUSADE OF CHARLES OF ANJOU

For the next 70-odd years, the papacy preached a series of crusades in Italy, most aimed at countering the power of Emperor Fredrick II and his Hohenstaufen descendants in Sicily. Most notable was the holy war waged in Sicily in 1265 by Charles of Anjou, brother of King Louis IX of France.

In 1254 Frederick II's illegitimate son Manfred seized power in Sicily and declared himself regent, then entered an alliance with the Saracens to defeat a papal army at Foggia. Pope Alexander IV (ruled 1254–61) excommunicated Manfred, and his successor, Urban IV (ruled 1261–64), offered the crown of Sicily to Charles of Anjou. Urban's successor, Clement IV

▲ *This coin was issued by the Ghibelline government of Genoa, northern Italy.*

(ruled 1265–68), had Charles declared King of Sicily in Rome in May 1265. Charles led his army on campaign and defeated and killed Manfred at the Battle of Benevento on 26 February 1266 to become King of Sicily.

WARS OF THE SICILIAN VESPERS

Charles was driven out of Sicily in 1282 and the people allied themselves with the royal house of Aragon. Almost 20 years of fighting followed, known as the Wars of the Sicilian Vespers (1283–1302), and in this period the papacy called a series of crusades to restore Angevin rule. None of these crusades succeeded.

CRUSADES OF AN EXILED PAPACY

In 1305, the papacy established itself in France. Through the period of the papacy's French exile (until 1378), various popes in exile declared crusades against the Ghibellines in Italy, but none succeeded.

During the ensuing Great Papal Schism of 1378–1417, the two sides used crusades against one another with no success. After this date, the holy war as an instrument of papal policy was little seen, found only occasionally in the 16th century under popes such as Julius II. The age of the crusade was finally over.

INDEX

▲ *Frederick, Holy Roman Emperor, 1220.*

▼ *Frederick, Holy Roman Emperor, 1220.*